# PERFIDY

## The Government Cabal That Knowingly Abandoned Our Prisoners of War And Left Them to Die

By John Top Holland

and

Father Patrick Bascio

# PERFIDY:

## *The Government Cabal That Knowingly Abandoned Our Prisoners of War And Left Them to Die*

First U.S. Printing: April 2008

Published by:    American Free Press
645 Pennsylvania Avenue, SE, Suite 100
Washington, D.C. 20003
1-888-699-6397
www.americanfreepress.net

ISBN #0-9785733-6-6 • ISBN # 978-0-9785733-6-2



To contact the authors email:

**John Top Holland**
topholland@yahoo.com

**Father Patrick Bascio**
pajbascio@yahoo.com

# TABLE OF CONTENTS:

# PERFIDY

# The Brotherhood

"I now know why men who have been to war yearn to reunite. Not to tell stories or look at old pictures. Not to laugh or weep. Comrades gather because they long to be with the men who once acted at their best; men who suffered and sacrificed, who were stripped of their humanity. I did not pick these men. They were delivered by fate and the military. But I know them in a way I know no other men. I have never given anyone such trust. They were willing to guard something more precious than my life. They would have carried my reputation, the memory of me. It was part of the bargain we all made, the reason we were so willing to die for one another. As long as I have my memory, I will think of them all, every day. I am sure that when I leave this world, my last thought will be of my family and my comrades. . . . Such good men."

—AUTHOR UNKNOWN

# Background on the 'Select Committee'

On August 2, 1991, the United States Senate approved a resolution introduced by Sen. Robert Smith providing for the creation of a Select Committee on POW/MIA Affairs to serve during the remainder of the 102nd Congress. In October, 1991, a chairman (Sen. John Kerry), Co-chairman (Sen. Robert Smith), and 10 additional members were appointed to the committee. The hearings began on November 5, 1991. The Committee's Final Report was issued on January 13, 1993. The Committee's task was to investigate the events, policies, and knowledge that guided U.S. Government POW/MIA-related actions over the previous 20 years. Because of the private agendas of a few men on the Committee, its Report was not honest and those who contributed to the dishonesty are not honorable men.

**JOHN TOP HOLLAND** entered the Marines after the attack on Pearl Harbor. He served in Korea and Vietnam as well. He has worked tirelessly for decades to rescue those veterans who have been abandoned by the U.S. government. He is the president of Concerned Citizens for Known But Abandoned POWs, P.O. Box 305, Moores Hill, IN 47032. Email: knownbutabandonedpows@yahoo.com.

# ACKNOWLEDGMENTS

We would like to thank those POW/MIA activists and helpers who gave advice and information to Fr. Pat as he assembled our book. We would like to mention: Joe Oliver, Tynan Brown, author, Robert and Bill Dumas, Dean Bernal, Bobby Garwood, Barbara Burchim, Patty Hopper, Denese Denman (for editing), Sue Hurst (for editing), Gary Puckett (for podcast interviews), Pat and Charlene Holland (for their computer expertise), Josh Holland, (for his computer expertise), Major Mark Smith, for his contribution, Van Loman, journalist, for recommending this work to the publisher, and Joyce Ussery.

## PEOPLE WHO INSPIRE ME

If I had to point to any one person who gave me inspiration to even attempt this book project, it would have to be Father Pat Bascio, my co-author and researcher for this book. Several of my fellow activists, whose abilities and opinions I cherish, had previously offered to help me. However, Father Pat's encouragement, from a person who initially had absolutely no knowledge of the Issue, "tipped the scale." He listened to me talk about the subject and he only about half-believed me. He then researched my information, found me credible in what he calls "my knowledge and opinions," and offered to help me in my efforts.

There are so many people who have taken part in trying to alert the American People of the POW/MIA Issue, and each of them offered their hearts, their time, and their hard earned money. They do this not for vindication of their beliefs but for their American sense of values and justice. A list of people who inspire me would be endless. I can start with the HUNDREDS OF THOUSANDS of bikers and friends who attend "Rolling Thunder" each Memorial Day Weekend in Washington, D.C. They are a true representation of how the American People feel about the POW/MIA Issue.  A few of the others are:

- Col. Earl Hopper Sr., USA, Ret. WWII, Korea & Vietnam veteran, father of Abandoned POW.
- Patty Hopper, Issue activist, analyst, author, and director of TFO.
- Master Sergeant Ray Bows, USA Ret., Vietnam veteran, author & Issue advocate.
- Chris Noel, civ. Vietnam vet, actress, veteran advocate, Issue activist.
- Dave Teke, Vietnam veteran, Issue activist.
- Chief Master Sergeant Ray Sutherland USAF Ret., Vietnam veteran, Issue activist.
- Judi Sutherland, radio talk show hostess, Issue activist.
- Artie Muller, Vietnam vet, Director, Rolling Thunder, Issue activist.
- Sgt Diana Jones, USA Ret., Desert Storm veteran, Issue activist.
- Congressman John Rowland, Issue advocate, MSPA '95 initiator.
- Ted Shpak, Vietnam veteran, Issue activist, lobbyist.
- John Malloy, Vietnam veteran, retired bank vice president, Issue activist, director Vietnam Veterans Coalition.
- Tom Birch, Vietnam vet, VA Counsel, Issue activist, past director Vietnam Veteran Coalition.
- Ted Sampley, Vietnam veteran, Issue activist, editor, U.S. government agent provocateur.
- Steve Kiba, Korean War veteran, two years abandoned POW in China, author.
- John Noble (deceased), WWII civilian detainee four years, 10 yrs abandoned civilian in USSR.
- Bobby Garwood, Vietnam veteran, 14 years abandoned POW in Vietnam, Issue activist.
- Mike Bentz, civilian Vietnam veteran, ex-POW, Issue activist.
- Larry Stark, civilian Vietnam veteran, ex-POW, Issue activist.
- Senator Bob Smith (R-N.H.) retired, Vietnam veteran, Issue activist, brought Issue to Senate floor.
- Bob Dumas, Korean War veteran, brother of abandoned POW in

Korea, Issue activist.
  • Carol Hrlicka, wife of abandoned POW in Laos, Issue activist.
  • Anne Holland (no relation to the author), wife of abandoned POW in Laos, Issue activist.
  • Larry Humble, son of abandoned WWII POW in the USSR, Issue activist.
  • Joe & Mary Milliner, parents of abandoned POW in Laos, Issue activists.
  • Sara Nichols, Issue activist.
  • Sharon Jones, Vietnam veteran, Issue activist.
  • Carla Wetzel, director of Freedom Fest, Issue activist.
  • Major Mark Smith, U.S. Army, Special Forces, Vietnam veteran, POW, Issue activist, retired.
  • Danny Belcher, Vietnam veteran, director TFO-KY.
  • My seven children, Issue activists all.
  • Diane Thompson, Issue activist.
  • Denese Denman, Issue advocate, proofreader extraordinaire.
  • Sammy Davis, U.S. Army Ret., (CMH-Recpt.).
  • Mike Martin, Vietnam veteran, musician, Issue activist.
  • Tynan Brown, Issue activist.
  • Monica Jensen Stevenson, Issue activist and POW/MIA author.

Thanks to All,
JOHN TOP HOLLAND

**U.S. Marine Sgt. Tim Chambers** salutes as bikers riding in the Memorial Day annual Ride for Freedom XVI, pass by in Washington, D.C. The annual massive motorcycle parade aims at increasing awareness about abandoned U.S. Prisoners of War. It is sponsored by Rolling Thunder, Inc. Sgt. Chambers stood at attention and saluted the participants for two hours, saying afterward "It's what I can do" to show appreciation for their efforts.

DAVID S. HOLLOWAY/AFP/GETTY IMAGES

# CHAPTER ONE

# JOHN HOLLAND REFLECTS ON THE STRUGGLE

I HAVE BEEN ENCOURAGED BY THE POW/MIA COMMUNITY to see that this book was written in order to record a bit of history of the epic battle fought between the POW/MIA activists and the U.S. Government during a period when I was actively involved. This was during the 1980's and 1990's. I shall also tell how a person, with absolutely no experience in politics or lobbying, can actually initiate a change in law and encourage a large group of activists to successfully change a long-standing law that had been flawed since its inception in 1942. At the time I started this odyssey, I didn't even know I was making one. Usually, a trip to visit your brother does not morph into a life-changing event that affects the lives of thousands of people. I did not go to the Washington, D.C. area with any intent of being involved in any form of protest or issue. My sole reason in going was to spend some time with my younger brother, a retired Air Force Master Sergeant, with whom I had spent very little time in the previous thirty years. I had no inkling that I would become embroiled in the POW/MIA Issue. One contact led to another, and soon many people in the POW/MIA community voiced the thought that I should write about the struggle that we shared, seeking the truth about our missing comrades and family members. Members of the POW/MIA community asked me to tell the story of how I questioned and changed the law under which Missing Service Personnel were declared dead, that I should make public the troubles, trials, and tribulations I had initially faced alone, as I struggled to rectify a law I deemed to be the cause of the entire POW/MIA problem.

After reading his book, *Defeating Islamic Terrorism: The Wahhabi Factor,* I sought the assistance of Father Patrick Bascio. I explained to him the nature and background of the difficulties facing the POW Community's attempt to discover the truth in the Government's handling of issues facing the POW community. That conversation led to a decision that we would collaborate on a book exposing the truth. I would provide the fruit of my own experience, memories and contacts; he would provide his writing and investigative skills. This book is the fruit of that decision.

My story goes back to my early visits to Washington, D.C. I started alone, but the work soon mushroomed into groups from Maine to California, groups determined to get at the truth. The task became one supported by POW/MIA family members, every concerned veteran, and thousands of other citizens. After many visits to Congressional offices, we also received support from a few dedicated members of Congress and the Senate. Yes, we finally succeeded in getting some changes made in the law pertaining to this issue, but the troubles, trials, and tribulations have not abated. The issue still exists and continues to haunt our nation, as it has since World War II. The POW/MIA Issue will not go away by itself, and it will continue until the entire government faces the fact that we are a nation of laws, and these laws were written to protect the people of this nation, not just elected or appointed officials. It is my belief that the POW/MIA Issue may have started with the gross incompetence of certain senior military officers and State Department officials, and their fear of being exposed as incompetent and insensitive fools. There was also the fear that some top officials of our government would, at the least, be embarrassed by details that might emerge. Once started down this slimy, slippery slope, it became easier, with each succeeding war, to abandon thousands more of our Missing Personnel. This criminal farce became even more necessary as the reputations of some men, known to the public as great statesmen, military heroes, and "peacemakers," were jeopardized. Some of them had advanced to very high positions in our government. Had the truth been told, the "clay feet" of some "great statesmen" would have become exposed, and who knows how history might have been altered? I do believe that many thousands of American Service Personnel were abandoned to our enemies, in part to save and even advance the careers of these personages and those who collaborated with them. Our American POWs suffered slow and agonizing deaths while our government (knowing this and knowing exactly where many of them were!) did nothing at all to gain their release. We in the POW/MIA community worked for many years to change the law, so that our government would be pressured into taking seriously their own words: "We leave no men behind." Certain elected officials, in both houses of Congress, have aided and abetted in this, at times, criminal behavior. Some of these elected officials have gone so far as to change laws, to the detriment of POWs/MIAs, without the knowledge of the rest of Congress. By dishonorably misusing a system that relies on honor, both houses of Congress have been dishonored. They have stymied justice for our Missing Personnel and thus stymied justice for all of us.

The law that I was instrumental in changing was the Missing Persons Act of 1942 (MPA 42). This was a fiscal law under which the pay and allowances of Missing Personnel was controlled, and under which the status of Missing personnel could be changed to "dead." Had I thought about it previously, I would have begun this work of finding the truth much earlier, but I was an Infantryman and considered that far above my pay grade and expertise. My duties had consisted of training to fight, training others to fight, and fighting. I had spent my life in the Infantry, not as an REMF (rear echelon) pencil pusher or a bean counter.

I am a retired U.S. Army Sergeant Major with more than twenty-six years of active duty, all of it as a Regular. I am proud to have served as a combat Infantryman in the three wars, varying from a U.S. Marine in WW II, Paratrooper in Korea, and member of Special Forces in Vietnam. I first enlisted in the U.S. Marines one month after Pearl Harbor, I was only fourteen, but pretended otherwise. I served over eighteen months in the South Pacific (1942 -1944) as an Automatic Rifle Man. I first saw action in the mop-up of Guadalcanal and I was in the first wave during the landing on Bougainville. I was evacuated home with severe malaria, filarisis, and "combat fatigue." I vehemently disagreed with that last diagnosis. Eventually, I was discharged with a Medical Discharge and eighty percent disability. I reckon the Navy thought I was really crazy, or something, because right to the day of my discharge I argued to stay in and go back to the Pacific. I knew I did not have combat fatigue. In fact I had rather gloried in combat for the good of my country, until I got so sick I couldn't properly participate.

During the next two years I tried on numerous occasions to enlist. I tried the Marines, the Army, and the Navy, but to no avail: As soon as they saw my discharge I was disqualified. My discharge stated very plainly that it was an Honorable Discharge, but the regulations disqualified me from reenlisting. I became getting desperate. I had my heart set on being a Soldier, and that was all I ever wanted to be. Finally I devised a plan. My younger brother turned eighteen in August of 1947, so I made a point to be in Indianapolis on that date. I easily got a copy of his birth certificate, and I enlisted immediately. Yes, under his name. My plan was "if I am caught, I will probably get a year or so at Leavenworth, after which I can go to France and join the Foreign Legion." I wanted to be in Uncle Sam's service, but if not, I would still be a soldier. I also thought that if I could pull a full enlistment, I would be able to reenlist under my own name. I had been in the service about two months when my mother read in the local paper that her youngest son, "Robert," was taking Basic Training in the Army. She knew better, because he was sitting across the table from her, eating breakfast. Years later, Bob told me that Mom put two and two together, and said, "I know where John Rufus is." Mom informed the Army. Mom was still trying to help save me from myself. (Mom had tried to get me out of the Marines when I was sixteen, but a kindly Marine General got me a waiver.) For some reason the Army granted another waiver. I got my real name back and was even given credit for my Marine service. I did not go before a board of any kind. To this day I don't know how or why I received the waiver, and I never asked. (As a kid I learned, "Never look a gift horse in the mouth; he might bite you.")

In 1950 I reenlisted for six years and went to Korea with 187th Airborne Regimental Combat Team (187th) and fought as a Squad Leader and Assistant Platoon Sergeant. I returned to the states for a year or so and then to Germany for the better part of four years. I reenlisted several more times and volunteered for Special Forces. I served my first two tours in Vietnam (1963 -1965) as a Special Forces Team Sergeant. My third tour I was the Battalion Sergeant Major of an Infantry Battalion (4th Bn 39th Inf) in the 9th Infantry Division (1967 -1969). My fourth tour (1969-1970) I served as the Senior Enlisted Advisor for the 2nd Vietnamese Infantry Division (2nd Arvn). After I had been discharged from the Marines, I reenrolled in my old high school. I was accepted as a sophomore and attended school for a year. In 1946 the high school GED test had become law, so I took the test and received my high school diploma with the class of '46. While on active duty, I had taken a few college courses, whenever I could, but it was very difficult to fit night school into an Infantry NCO's schedule. After I retired, in August 1970, I started taking more college classes, and I eventually received two Associate Degrees. But, what I was most satisfied about was that I had already spent my life being exactly what I wanted to be—a soldier!

In July 1982 I went to the Washington, DC area and visited my brother for a couple of weeks. While I was there I found a job I thought I might enjoy for a while, and decided to move there. My wife and I had separated about two years after I had retired (we learned that we got along real well together, as long as we were apart). We still had small children at home and I supported our family with my retirement pay, which was actually more than most working people made in that part of Indiana. Shortly after arriving in Washington, I visited the Vietnam Veterans Memorial before it was completed. One day I made my way through the construction workers and stood by first panel, 01E, reading the names listed on it, covering the years 1959 through mid-1965. I was amazed at the number of names I recognized. As I was gazing at the names, seeing faces and places of long ago, reliving conversations, miseries, and laughs we had shared for so many years, I was deeply affected. A young man, who stood next to me, asked if I thought the public would like the memorial. In answering, I told him I loved it because it gives the men whose names appear here the appreciation they rightly deserve. It wasn't until much later that I learned that I, in a "left handed manner," had given Jan Scruggs (the initiator of the wall's construction) some assurance that he needed at the time.

When the Vietnam Veterans Memorial was dedicated, I spent every waking hour of those three days at the ceremonies just hanging around. I met people I had not seen for years, and I met people of whom I had only heard. I enjoyed more camaraderie than I had known since I had retired. It was a wonderful feeling. I had not realized how much I had missed being around people who had the same interests as I. In spite of this, the following month or so were some of the worst days I had ever had in my life. I went into a fit of depression the likes of which I had never known. The only way I can explain it is that all three wars came down on me at the same time. I even missed several days of work, just sitting in my living room with the TV turned off. I went home to Indiana for a week to take care of a little business and see the kids that were still home, but I was still down-in-the-dumps when I returned to DC. I had quit drinking more than three years before I went into this fit of depression. Then I nearly convinced myself drinking would help me get over the blues. However, I still had enough sense to seek help. For the first time in my life I went to AA. It wasn't a cure, but it helped me over the really rough places. I am now twenty-nine years dry!

I had long been aware of the POW/MIA Issue and I personally knew men in all three wars who remained Missing. My sister's brother-in-law, Howard Humble, was declared Missing during the Battle of the Bulge. The Soviets had released him from a German POW camp in Dresden, Germany. Shortly thereafter, he was ordered to go to a Soviet dispensary for treatment of a minor ailment. It is believed that he is one of the 20,000 to 30,000 Americans, released from German POW camps by the Soviets and then moved to their notorious prison gulag. These Missing men were never to be seen again, and their absence has never been explained by the American government.

And then there was Morton Lee who, in 1945, was about fifteen. He followed me around like a lost puppy. I realized that he was a lot like me, old for his age and very interested in the military. We became friends and I tried to mentor him. When he was sixteen he wanted to quit school, but I talked him into staying in school a little longer. Then when he was seventeen I helped him convince his mother to allow him to join the Army. I saw him once after he enlisted. He was proud as punch, and very happy to be a soldier. He went to Japan with the occupation forces, and then to Korea to fight as an Infantryman. He went Missing along the Yalu River the first night the Chinese entered the war. He was rumored to be a POW, but he has never been released. Locally, he has been more or less forgotten by everyone except me, and one or two of his classmates. I had his name and status placed on a memorial brick at the County Memorial when it was dedicated a few years ago.

In Vietnam there were many missing personnel with whom I was acquainted and several I knew very well. One of them was a man I had served with in the 77th, 10th, and 5th Special Forces Groups, Ed Dodge. I had a beer with him a day or so before Christmas 1964. He went Missing that New Years Eve, while flying out to an A Team site. Many years later I saw a report, made by a defector who had been a prison guard. The defector definitely identified the pilot of the plane as a POW, and Ed as a probable POW. The defector's debriefing was dated more than five years after they went Missing. In 1973 neither my friend, nor the pilot, was released.

Christmas Eve 1982, a month or so after the Vietnam Veterans Memorial was dedicated, I was sitting alone, watching the eleven o'clock news, when there was blurb about a group of veterans who had started a Veterans Vigil for POWs/MIAs at the Victnam Veterans Memorial. By midnight I had joined them, and I remained with them until the afternoon of Christmas Day. The group that formed the Veterans Vigil had come from the Cleveland, Ohio area. I began to volunteer my time at the vigil, and about a hundred others from the vicinity of DC also began showing up. We were put on their schedule and became a part of the group. The vigil was working in conjunction with the "National League of Families of Men Missing in Southeast Asia" (the "League" or NLF), and they were passing out literature furnished by that organization. After a couple of months, some of the locals became disgruntled and started to melt away. I began to take on a few responsibilities of the group, even though I also had some misgivings about the overall management of the vigil. Then I was invited to go to a meeting with the local manager of the vigil at the offices of the NLF. This was where I first met Ms Ann Mills-Griffith, the director of the NLF. To be truthful, she rather impressed me with her knowledge and apparent dedication to the issue. I considered myself a guest at the meeting, so when I heard what I thought were intentional misstatements by the local manager, I didn't say anything. After we returned to the vigil site, I called him aside and asked him about what was said, and also I asked where the donated money was going. I couldn't get straight answers to my questions, so I quit on the spot. Several weeks later, I received a call from one of the local volunteers. He asked me if I would be interested in forming our own group and opening another vigil at the wall. I thought that might be a good idea, so we got about fifty or so of the locals together and formed The American Foundation For Accountability of POW/MIAs ("AFFA"). We were so bitter about the misuse of the donated funds at the vigil, that initially we would neither accept donations, nor sell anything. We decided to run the vigil from our own pockets, while working in conjunction with the NLF, who agreed to furnish literature and handouts to us. Shortly after AFFA began its "Watch" one of the Cleveland members of the vigil overdosed on heroin and died in one of the park restrooms. This incident confirmed what we believed had been happening to the money that was donated to the vigil. Shortly after this incident the vigil people folded their tents and slipped away in the night.

Chuck Eatley, another retired Sergeant Major, was elected president of AFFA and I was elected senior vice president. Chuck wasn't in the best of health, so most of the day-to-day management fell on me. We maintained our "watch" from the spring of

1983 until October when tourism fell away to nothing, and the weather became so miserable that most of our volunteers found other attractions to keep them busy. (That is were I learned the true meaning of "summertime soldiers"!) AFFA then began setting up only on weekends and special days. Meanwhile, I had been learning more and more about the issue and I had started asking questions no one could answer, or didn't want to answer. All the NLF wanted to talk about was the Missing men from the Vietnam era, and would not mention WWII or Korea. Their excuse was, "it [had] been such a long time." I wrote a handout discussing all three eras, and Ms Griffith said that if we passed it out, we could no longer use their literature. AFFA's board of directors agreed with me, so we informed Ms Griffith that as a separate organization we would choose our own subjects. (I believe that this made AFFA the first POW/MIA group to champion the abandoned servicemen from all eras.) We further informed the NLF that while we would not be working in close conjunction with them, we would continue to support their efforts. If the NLF would no longer furnish literature, we would make our own. This was when we started selling items. Even after AFFA began sales, we tried to be self supporting and we still refused to accept donations. Initially, I furnished the funds to purchase our sales items, and to publish our handouts, but soon AFFA was in the black. With the surplus cash we garnered, we began bringing in volunteers from around the country to help us work our booth. Then later, we started furnishing transportation and lodging to activists and family members who would testify before Congressional hearings, or lobby for passage of certain Congressional Bills. (Note: Anyone who volunteers to testify at a Congressional hearing must pay their own transportation to and from DC, and their own expenses while in DC.) It was the earnings from our sales that allowed AFFA to begin organizing and conducting demonstrations. It was also with these earnings that we conducted the first eight Rolling Thunder runs. AFFA welcomed other POW/MIA groups to participate in our activities, but AFFA paid all of the expenses

About 1984 I began to seriously wonder how the government

really decided that Missing Service Personnel were dead. I asked people who I thought should know, but I could not get a good answer. Finally, I went to the Capitol Building and bumbled around until I found an office that had copies of all of the laws. There I was able to get a copy of U.S. *Code Title 37 (Pay and Allowances of the Uniformed Services, Chapter 10—Payments to Missing Persons, Sections 551 through 558, known as the Missing Persons Act of 1942; MPA-42.* Shortly thereafter I visited the Army Personnel Office, in the Hoffman Building in Alexandria, Virginia, and requested a copy of the Army Regulations pertaining to Missing Service Personnel. I received a copy of Army Regulations (AR) 600-8-1, Chapter 10, dated 09/18/86. Having served under this law for more that twenty-six years, and having never thought about it, I belatedly learned that Missing Service Personnel are declared dead under a law that pertains to finance. The primary purpose of the act is to alleviate financial hardship suffered by dependents of personnel reported in a missing status (See Par 10-1 of AR 600-8-1 date 09/18/86). I found it strange that the welfare of the Missing Personnel is never mentioned in the law or the regulations. I later learned that since their welfare is never mentioned, it is never considered. The law made no prerequisite to seriously search for these personnel, nor is it written that the records of the opposing forces that held the area at the time of the incident must be checked. Thus, under this law no true investigation was ever initiated. Because of the manner in which this law was written (i.e. for the sole purpose of protecting the financial welfare of dependents), a gross injustice was foisted on the Missing Personnel and thus on the American Public as a whole. Prior to 1974 all Missing Service Personnel could be declared dead under this law, and no member of the family was allowed to attend any of the hearings pertaining to the matter. In 1974 a court case changed it a little, allowing financial dependents to attend the final hearing. However, other family members still could not attend. This faulty court decision did not affect hearings for personnel who did not have financial dependents. Even after the court case, no family member could attend any hearing pertaining to their loved one, unless they were financial dependents. This decision had a very detrimental effect when it came time for any hearing that pertains to the incident in which the Missing Service Person disappeared. Wives could attend, but parents and siblings could not. This was a great injustice.

We, the American people, have put up with this injustice for 50 years!

Why were the POW/MIA activists able to see and try to rectify this matter when thousands of government employees who had worked with it since its inception had done nothing to correct it? This is but one of the many malfeasances perpetrated by our government in its perfidious, deceitful abandonment of our Missing Service Personnel. Had I previously given thought to this subject, I would have first looked under the laws and regulations pertaining to all other personnel actions, not a finance law or regulation. To my way of thinking, (and I learned my thinking in the military) putting this responsibility in a finance law is like having the "tail wag the dog." The hearings pertaining to Missing Service Personnel should be treated as any other personnel hearing, and the finance laws and regulations should support the findings of the hearings, not direct how the hearings will be conducted! Compare the directions for the Missing Service Personnel hearings to the directions for all other hearings. The difference is plainly seen: THERE IS NO COMPARISON! The findings of other hearings cannot be directed as are the "after-the-war" mass declarations of "DEAD." Further, the decisions of all other hearings can be overturned by a commanding officer, or higher authority. UNDER THE MPA-42, NO ONE COULD OVER-RULE THE DECISIONS! NOT EVEN THE FEDERAL COURTS.

When I first read this law I became physically sick! How could MY Government do this to people who offer their all for this nation? How could the survivors of these Service Personnel be treated as if they had only furnished fodder for horses rather than the fact that they gave their lives or freedom for their country? I and my family had been susceptible to this mistreatment every time I offered myself on the altar of war! I read and reread this law and the regulations, mulling them over, time and again, trying to convince myself that I was misunderstanding them. It was a good while before I discussed it with anyone. I worried over it until I was sure that it was as wrong as I perceived it to be. Why did no one but me think this way? At that time, it had been written and used for more than forty years, and I was sure someone besides me had seen the deformity of the law. Someone should have done something about it many years ago. As alien as that thought was to a person with a background like mine, that was when I first started considering the possibility that the law may have been intentionally written to obfuscate the issue. I, a professional Infantry soldier, decided to try my best to set the government right. Yes, I considered the old adage, "Fools rush in where angels fear to tread." What would they do to me, send me back to Vietnam? All right! That's OK with me; I loved the place.

## HOLLAND BEGINS VISITING CONGRESS

I had already spoken to a few Navy captains and Army colonels, most of whom either had a family member among the Missing, or had been a POW themselves. I met them at issue meetings, but other than telling me about the court case in 1973 (that allowed dependents to attend the hearings) they all thought it would just be shoveling debris against the tide (an exercise in futility). They were convinced that even after a costly court case, only Congress can change laws. Not heeding their lack of interest, I began visiting the congressional office of any Congressman I could get into. I was green as grass. I had no idea of how to go about it. I would go into an office and occasionally I would get to speak to an aide, but no more. They would listen to me, or at least act like they listened, take the copy of the law I would give them, say they would speak to the congressman, and hustle me out the door. In my spare time, I did this for a few months. However, I spoke about it to no one in the movement.

Finally one aide took pity on me and explained the facts of life. He informed me that I had best get to know someone who knew someone who knew a congressman, and thus get a personal meeting through this friend of a friend. Still naïve, I thought it wasn't the way I believed it should work, but I figured that "When in Rome, . . ."I met Ted Shpak at the vigil, and he was also a member of AFFA. I traveled to Connecticut with Ted a time or two to visit a Veterans Outreach Program he had started. I also knew he had helped Congressman John Rowland (R-CT) get elected. I brought Ted up to date on what I had been doing, and he liked the idea of changing the law. I asked if he could get me in to see Congressman Rowland, and sure enough in about two weeks we had a meeting. At our first meeting Congressman Rowland expressed strong interest, but he stated that he would like to discuss it with another congressman or two.

A couple weeks later, Ted and I were called back to his office and were told to write the bill we wanted. That came as a total shock to me as neither Ted nor I had ever seen a congressional bill, let alone wrote one. Ted and I went back to AFFA's office and, with copies of a couple of other bills as guidance, we wrote what we thought would straighten out the "MPA 1942." It took us a couple of weeks to get the format as correct as we possibly could and the wording the way we wanted it. (We admitted to each other that it was probably a miserable bill.) The Congressman actually put the bill in as we had written it. It was late in that session of Congress, and we didn't expect it to pass, but as least we had a bill and the assurance that it would be re-introduced in the next session.

At the start of the next session, Congressman Rowland called us back and asked if we could get anyone to help us write a proper bill. With that, I contacted Tom Birch, a lawyer in DC (and a Vietnam Veteran who had been a Judge Advocate Officer for the 5th Special Forces Group). Tom had recently organized The Vietnam Veterans Coalition, a group of small Veterans organizations and several POW/MIA groups (of which AFFA was one). An associate of Tom, Bill Bennett, also a lawyer (and also a Vietnam Veteran) whose area of expertise is writing documents, agreed to go with me to the Capitol Building and do it up properly. Congressman Rowland got us into the area where most of the bills were written, and where information of all sorts is maintained. In three days we had the "Missing Service Personnel Act" (MSPA) written pretty much as I had envisioned it. Congressman

Rowland put the bill in the hopper immediately.

The MSPA received a lot of interest and wound up with nearly a hundred cosponsors. However, we could not get it into the Armed Forces Committee for consideration. After the session ended, we tried again in the next session, with the same results. All of the member groups, of the Vietnam Veterans Coalition, supported our efforts and most of them actively lobbied Congress with us.

During the second session that we had the bill, the National Headquarters of the American Legion got firmly behind us, and the Legion's efforts were strongly felt in Congress, but still to no avail. I approached the National Headquarters of the Veterans of Foreign Wars, but they showed no interest in it. The reason they did not help us was a question I could not answer for some time, and I still have only suspicions. Most individual VFW posts, around the country, as well as some states and districts, were very strong in their support, but National VFW helped us not.

## HOLLAND BILL GETS PASSED

Someone in Congress, or close to Congress, was stymieing the bill, but we didn't know who nor exactly why. We knew that the Defense Prisoners of War / Missing Personnel Office (DPMO) did not like it, and actively fought against it. That we could understand! Bureaucrats work in that office, some in uniform and some as civilians, and this act would not only cause them to have to work harder, but to also accept responsibility. After his third term, Congressman Rowland left Congress, and we did not immediately get another congressman to introduce it. However, later that session, Congressman Murphy (D-Pa.), decided to introduce it again, written exactly as Congressman Rowland had introduced it.

Believe it or not, Congressman Murphy introduced it in two sessions, in the same format, and it still was not accepted for consideration by the Armed Forces Committee, although each time we had over a hundred co-sponsors. Murphy then left Congress and the next congressman to pick it up was Congressman

Bob Dornan (R-CA). That same session, in 1994, Senators Bob Dole (R-KS) and Charles (Chuck) Grassley (R-IA) introduced a companion bill in the Senate, and we finally got the MSPA passed and signed by the president early in 1995.

The final law was not exactly what I had started out to get, but I knew it was as close as I would ever come. The law finally gave all family members the right to attend all of the hearings, and allowed the service personnel to designate someone besides a family member to represent them (naturally, they had to make such choice before they went Missing).

A missing service person could not be declared dead solely because of passage of time, until fifty years had passed.

For the first time, Missing American civilians accompanying the armed forces, under orders, in combat areas, would have their absences explained by the Defense Department, rather than be treated like wandering tourists by the State Department. Proof had to be given that the area where the missing service person disappeared had been searched, and, if the war was over, the records of the national power, or other element that had occupied that area at the time of the incident, had been searched for information pertaining to the incident. Rather than having one officer with no special qualifications, every hearing had to have a group of officers assigned to it, and they had to have certain qualifications, including a person qualified in the same field as the missing service person, and if the person was missing while in transit, there had to be a person on the board that was qualified in that type of transport.

Each Missing Service person was assigned legal representation and additional legal representation could be hired by the family if desired. All findings of the hearings could be appealed. Also there were punitive instructions for anyone who intentionally withheld information from the records of the individual missing persons. There were also provisions for survivors of Missing Personnel (going back to WW II) to request full hearings on their loved one's case.

Overall, it was a very good law, and it satisfied most every complaint that the Issue family members and activists had against the MPA of 42. There were no big announcements in the newspapers or on TV, like there is when the President signs some sort of law that gives the government more power. The fact that a bad law, that was responsible for long lasting problem of "great national interest," had finally been rectified was not noted by the national media. In retrospect, I know now that we should have called a press conference and had the Senators and Congressmen responsible for introducing the Act announce it to the public.

## MCCAIN CHICANERY

To be honest, we activists thought that the battle had been won, and we were the victors. I guess that it just goes to show exactly how naïve we still were. The Act was signed into law early in 1995, but, unknown to us, Senator John McCain introduced a Bill in February 1995 that gutted our law. Senator McCain's new Bill remained unknown to us for nearly a year before we learned about it from one of the few people in DPMO who was "friendly" to we activists and our subject. Senator McCain could get very few other Senators to co-sign his Bill, and no one in the House put in a companion Bill. Senator McCain finally got the Bill passed through what I believe is a very furtive method, even though it is considered legal. Normally, to pass a Bill into law, each house of Congress must vote on the Bill that is passed by each respective house. Seldom are these two Bills written exactly the same in their language. Once the two companion Bills are passed, they must go to what is called a "Conference Committee," which is where a number of chosen Congressmen and a number of chosen Senators discuss the Bills. They then re-write the Bill to include as much of each individual Bill as they decide should be included in the final Bill. This final Bill then goes back to each House, where it is again given a vote, but the vote is either yes or no, and no additions, no reductions to the Bill can be introduced. In fact, very few of these final Bills are ever read by the majority of the two houses, as they rely on the original Bill as it was passed.

This method is understandable because otherwise nothing would ever get done. However, there is "a fly or two in the ointment." The Conference Committee has the right to add anything they wish to the Bill, and it will be passed by both Houses without discussion. However (and here is where "Honor" comes into play) a person of contemptible nature can slip into the final Bill any other piece of legislation that he knows will not bear discussion by the individual committees, or the entire Congress. (In fact, this is how most earmarks are inserted) I have heard, from people who should know, that even the other members of the Conference committee did not know that Senator John McCain had added his Bill (the one that gutted the MSPA) to the Bills they were discussing. In light of what happened next, I firmly believe this.

## MORE MCCAIN CHICANERY

As soon as we learned about Senator McCain, acting alone, OVERRODE BOTH HOUSES OF CONGRESS, we went to Congressman Dornan, who immediately put in House Resolution 4000, which would override McCain's nefarious activities. The year was 1996, and it was the last day of the Congressional Session, with Congressional Elections coming in a month or so. At the end of a Congressional Session, it is possible to pass a Bill in what is called "cloture." If a Bill is passed in one House of Congress, and it passes with no one voting "nay," it goes immediately to the other House, where, if it is written in the exact wording as the Bill that passed in the first House, and again it passes with no one voting "nay" it is ready for the President's signature. Thus, when a Bill is passed, in cloture, in both Houses, it does not go to a Conference Committee. HR 4000 passed the House of Representatives 410 to 0, and the Senate was waiting for it to reach the floor, where arrangements had been made to get quick approval of all of the Senators. But, something happened! It never reached the Senate floor. Remember, all it took to stop this cloture bill from passing, and going to the President to be signed into law, was for one Senator to stand up and say "No." But as I said, it never reached the floor. Why? I did not learn the reason for about two months when a "little bird" told me to read the *Congressional Record* for, I believe, September 23, 1996, or a date close to that. Why did it not reach the floor, where Senator McCain could have stopped it by publicly voting "No"? Remember, that one little vote would have exposed Senator McCain to be the enemy of the POW/MIA Issue that we activists had long believed him to be. He had clandestinely submitted not one, but two long amendments to this Bill, thus shutting it off from the cloture vote! Remember, the wording had to be exactly the same on both Bills. Rather than expose himself to public scorn by voting "No," he sneakily by-passed the entire Senate and the entire House of Representatives, and in so doing he flaunted his position as a U.S. Senator and 'thumbed his nose' at the entire electorate! ALL OF US! If we the people are not his boss, who does he work for?

The fact of the matter is, his chicanery does not stop here! Within a year he pulled the same stunt and got away with it again. This time it was against his fellow ex-POWs! Do the other Senators have to accept part of the blame for what he has done? I believe they do. In a continuing 'show of unity,' all Senators jointly (but sometimes grimly) 'protect fellow Senators at all cost.' I believe they go far beyond what is acceptable to the American people! I believe this method would end if the American public were made clear on how it works. Until Senator McCain snuck another of his notorious 'stealth' bills through a Conference Committee the initial post-release statements of all ex-POWs had been open for public scrutiny, as are all government documents that are (and should not be) classified. After McCain's bill was passed, the only person who can see these statements is the ex-POWs himself, and he is not allowed to make copies of them, or even have with him a means to write down what he is reading. Since Senator John McCain went against the public laws, and common sense, all of these original debriefings are now classified FOR EVER!

How could such a Bill have been made into law? It is illegal to classify any information 'forever.' Under our laws, all classified documents are to be reviewed on a regular basis, and classification must be reduced after a given length of time (with certain exceptions for National Defense secrecy). Furthermore, why should any statement made by an ex-POWs be classified? For sure, the enemy who held them already held that knowledge. Again, the enemy already knows what the ex-POWs know and can make it public anytime they wish. The sole purpose of classifying any government document is to ensure that it does not reach the hands of an enemy. There is no authorization to classify anything just to keep it out of the hands of the American public.

A little aside here. I have worked many years with classified documents, and at one time I was very familiar with the laws and regulations that govern why they are classified and how they should be handled. I have never seen nor heard of authority to classify a document simply because it might embarrass someone. Documents that contain 'embarrassing information' are usually kept out of the distributions system and handled with discretion. Normally, such documents are hand-delivered to whomever they are intended. One must wonder: did John McCain take advantage of his position in the Senate to ensure that no one ever looks at his initial debriefing statement, made after his return from a POW prison in Vietnam? Did he admit to making radio broadcasts for the North Vietnamese? There is certainly a widespread belief that he did. Did he admit to breaking the Code of Conduct for U.S. POWs? He did on more than one occasion. Did he admit to accepting favors for giving information that he should not have given? It is another well-known, but unspoken fact, that he offered to give information for proper medical care. Did he offer up information about the Order of Battle of the U.S. Forces? (Order of Battle information is knowledge of where certain service personnel are, and what capabilities certain units or ships have). This is another widely shared belief.

Shortly after Sen. McCain used his position to undercut the efforts of POW families and activists and the will of the American people, I became very sick with heart and other physical problems. Again I had to leave the field of battle. As before, fear of the enemy did not "run me off." I had become ineffective due to ill ness, but I would soon be ready to reenter the fray.

There have been other Issue Bills go through Congress, but

the MSPA is still as it became after McCain's stealth bill. The portions of the MSPA that were left in the law have been responsible for Captain Spiecer (MIA in Desert Storm since 1991) having his status changed from dead back to MIA, and it has been responsible for Matt Maupin not being declared dead (MIA in Iraq since 2003). I am now healthy enough to again start thinking about the Issue and McCain's actions, but still I am not physically able to resume where I left off. Hopefully, by collaborating with Father Pat in writing this book I can rekindle the fire in the hearts of other concerned citizens and get action started to undo McCain's damage.

For whom does John McCain work? To whom is he responsible? If we can answer those questions we can settle the POW/MIA Issue in a manner that ensures that our nation will never again be faced with such a disgrace as the MSP 42 brought. One last thought about the POW/MIA Issue, John McCain is not the only villain! No, he is not the sole person responsible for the failure of our government to properly explain the absences of our Missing Service Personnel. The POW/MIA Issue was an old scandal long before he came onto the scene. There were, and are, many 'highly respected' individuals, many of whom are dead, who were, and are, responsible for this scandalous fiasco. Reputations of such dastardly people should not be considered. Their stellar reputations are based on lies and misrepresentations. They caused the imprisonment of innocent people, for long periods of time, and undoubtedly caused the early deaths of many, just as they will cause a slow lingering death for most of the remainder. At this date, there is a probability that a few still live in various countries where they have been imprisoned all of these years. We must bring all living Americans home, and punish those who caused and supported such misery and pain to the personnel they have abandoned.

In this chapter you have seen me grow from a happy, devil-may-care, retired soldier to a very concerned citizen. I could have very easily "rested on my laurels" as a three-war Infantry veteran and lived a long care-free life. However, I have freely dedicated the remainder of my existence to resolving this Issue, and in doing so, I will do my utmost to get our government back to what I have been taught (and firmly believe) it should be:

We are a nation of laws, and these laws should be written to makc our government a clear and open book so all can see and understand its daily operations.

Before we move on to Chapter Two, let us introduce you to Sammy Davis.

## SAMMY DAVIS AND FORREST GUMP

Sammy Davis received the Medal of Honor after serving in the Vietnam War and carrying three of his fallen comrades to safety. In March 1967, Davis was in Vietnam. He is one of only 111 living recipients of the award. In the movie, Forrest Gump, the actual footage of him receiving the Medal of Honor from President Lyndon B. Johnson was used, with Forrest Gump's (Tom Hanks') face superimposed on Sammy's face. Sammy served as a cannoneer in the Vietnam War. On Nov. 18, 1967, his battery came under heavy mortar attack, and he was thrown with his howitzer gun into a foxhole. Despite a broken back and crushed ribs, Davis carried three of his comrades across a river to the safety of the fire support base. President Johnson decorated Davis with the Medal of Honor exactly one year and one day later. His Medal of Honor was stolen in July 2005, but was recovered four days later.

And as you can see in the email below Sammy sent to Father Pat, the speech given by Forest Gump, was a modified version of the speech given by Sammy at the Mall, in Washington. The government folks present that day forbade Sammy to give his speech, claiming it would cause unrest, so, with the help of others, John Holland went ahead, wired him up, and he gave the speech anyway.

The speech was not given, as in the movie, on the front steps of the Lincoln Memorial. It was given, actually, on the steps to the Reflection Pool. John Holland had the permit, so as the Park Police talked to him about disconnecting the electrical connection to Sammy's speaker system, John protested and produced the permit he had received to use that very electrical outlet.

Then, the Park Police backed off and allowed me to make the connection.

Sammy made his speech.

Here is Sammy's email to Father Pat, Date: Mon, 18 Jun 2007:

> From: "Sammy l. Davis C.M.H."
> cudgel67@frtci.net
> To: "pat bascio" pajbascio@yahoo.com

> Fr. Pat:
> One of the significant issues about the Freedom Now speech. If you have seen the movie *Forrest Gump*. . . .
> When Forrest is on the mall in Washington D.C., preparing to speak to all the Veterans gathered, it was the Freedom Now speech that I actually gave. People from the government (ask John Holland who they were) said they would not allow the speech to be given because it would cause great concern among the people. . . . John Holland and others helped secure the electrical outlets all over the park . . . and, in fact the Freedom Now speech was given . . . but in the movie—it was portrayed as some in the government wanted it to be . . .

## SAMMY DAVIS—MEDAL OF HONOR RECIPIENT

Here is the text of Sammy's famous Washington, D.C. Mall speech, *Freedom Now*.

## FREEDOM NOW!

In 1963, 250,000 people were drawn to our nation's capital by a promise that was spoken in two words; two words that have gone on to shape the very soul of this nation, two words which expressed a concept so simple, so basic, yet so far away from life, as it was at that time, that the two words changed history. Those two words MUST be spoken again. We have dedicated a statue honoring our living that has been placed in the shadow of a monument honoring our dead. I suggest to you that the words of 1963 speak directly to those of us today who have yet to find a place on this mall.

Freedom Now!

Freedom now for the Prisoners of War and the Missing in Action who are yet to be "ACCOUNTED FOR" from the Vietnam War. Accounted for is a contemptible term to begin with—money and property are "accounted for," not men, "accounted for" is simply unacceptable!! It is unacceptable to even think that men are still imprisoned from a war that is no longer being fought. It is unacceptable that families have sent sons, brothers, and husbands to serve their Country and got question marks in return . . . it is " UNACCEPTABLE" that the business of nations cannot allow the pain of the unknown to Haunt them to the point of action.

The Reverend Martin Luther King brought pain and suffering into the face of a nation and he demanded that it be healed. He insisted that a nation born of justice and equality for all extend that justice to all citizens . . . He refused to accept that America had left anyone behind in chains and simply went about its business.

And he said TWO WORDS—FREEDOM NOW—which became a cry for justice, a cry for decency, a cry for fairness. For the mother of a Prisoner of War who cries every time she sees his photo   FREEDOM NOW. For the sons and daughters of the miss ing in action who do not remember what it feels like to be HUGGED by their FATHER—FREEDOM NOW! There have been promises enough that there will be action and there have been all too many guarantees of results that have NOT been followed through on . . .

If campaign promises of a renewed, stronger America are to be believed, it is up to U.S. to ensure that our past be settled. . . . An organizer of Dr. King's march of 1963 was asked, somewhat rhetorically, why the march ended at the reflecting pool and did not continue on to the steps of the Capitol building. . . . He said, "It's simple, man." The organizer replied. "The man in the White House can hear us from here" . . . The man in the White House—who already claims to support our goals—can hear you from here as well . . . FREEDOM NOW!

# CHAPTER TWO

# THE PROBLEM

**DAVID HALBERSTAM, PULITZER PRIZE-WINNING** author who covered the Vietnam War in the early 1960s, was perhaps the first American who began to uncover the many government cover-ups during and after the Vietnam War. President Kennedy once approached *The New York Times* in a White House meeting in October 1963, attempting to get Halberstam to back off his inquisitive and honest reporting. Kennedy suggested that Halberstam's boss, *New York Times* publisher Arthur Ochs Sulzberger, remove him from the Vietnam assignment, a suggestion Sulzberger rejected out-of- hand. This book is about some government officials, agencies and members of Congress who have been guilty of acting against the interests of POWs/MIAs and their families by blocking information that could have led to POWs/MIAs returning home. It is about their making no attempt to serve the heartbreaking interests of POW/MIA families by using their authority to declassify essential documentation. And, in a few cases, officials and a few Congressmen actually participated in either the destruction of essential documents or failed to report such destruction to the proper authorities.

In addition, at least one senator, John McCain, actively undermined legislation proposed by POW/MIA activists, countering favorable legislation, such as the bill John Holland guided along to enactment by the Congress. There are many names connected with the POW/MIA Issue, lots of blame to go around, but it is simply a fact, not an accusation, that the most prominent name associated with the POW/MIA controversy is Senator John McCain.

This book is about a lot more than John McCain but he does

continue to weave in and out of the narrative, both because of his actions and his inactions relative to the POW/MIA Issues. Americans are fully aware that if there is one rallying cry that unites us it is the care and treatment of our military, especially American Prisoners of War. This fact is the spare political ammunition that every politician carries in his knapsack to be used whenever he is in trouble or to shore up a flagging popularity. Senator Kerry, Co-Chairperson of the Senate Select Committee that held hearings into POW/MIA affairs, had this to say referring to those who had access to POW/MIA information: "I ask you and anyone else who has that kind of information—and you can hold this Senator and Senator Smith accountable, and I am sure you will if something happens . . ."

Well, today we are holding Sen. Kerry and the other collaborating members of the Committee who have been accused of hiding much of the truth, accountable. Not all government servants were corrupt on this Issue. Supporting discovery were honest men like Sen. Smith and Sen. Grassley. To them we offer our profound gratitude. The stated purpose of the special Senate committee—which convened in mid-1991 and concluded in January 1993—was to investigate the location and condition of POWs left behind.

Obviously, this should have been the goal of the Co-Chairmen of the Committee, but it clearly was not. Senator Kerry and his buddy John McCain had a private agenda that did not include speaking the truth. Anyone reading the Senate Hearing text could not possibly conclude that "there is no compelling evidence that POW's remain in captivity." Why would two wealthy men, having served in the military and having become prominent United States Senators, demean and dishonor themselves by purposely and diligently work for normalization with the Vietnamese torturers? The full story remains unknown, but there is a lot of evidence to explain part of the story.


## THE NIXON STATEMENT

President Nixon did the POW/MIA Issue a great disservice with his statement in 1973 that that all our POWs had been returned. Senator Daschle, on September 9, 1992, made this statement. "From my perspective, and listening to the data and reading the documents, there was a sea change [in] attitude immediately following the President's assertion that everybody has now come home." Since the Commander-in-Chief made this categorical statement, what incentive was there left for government agencies to continue the task and duty of finding and retrieving our POWs? That presidential statement signaled the death knell of the POW/MIA search.

## HISTORICAL ODDITY

One cannot read the testimony given at the Senate Select Committee hearings in the early 1990s without being overwhelmed by the fact that there was an abundance of evidence available. However, the evidence was either dismissed as irrelevant or denied to the POW family members and the press.  The historical oddity is that the two senators who most aggressively concluded that this abundance of evidence did not prove anything were the two senators that, from their own personal experience, knew better and should have been on the side of the servicemen and their families. McCain and Kerry were the two senators that POW/MIA families counted on the most, but their actions stunned and horrified them. For example, McCain described Navy Capt. Eugene "Red" McDaniel (Ret.) as "a fraud and a dishonorable man who preys upon the families of those still unaccounted for in the war." In contrast, journalist Monika Jensen-Stevenson described McDaniel as "one of the most tortured Americans in the history of war." It appears that McCain's famous vitriolic language was unleashed on McDaniel for another reason. McDaniel had committed, in McCain's eyes, the unpardonable offense of drafting a letter urging that the United States not lift the embargo on Vietnam until they provided a full accounting of all American POW/MIAs. The letter was signed by fifty of his fellow Ex-POWs. McCain's actions stunned these good men and their families. McCain has referred to POW/MIA families as "whiners and vultures, and lunatic fringe." Now why in the name of all that is good and sane would any American use an expression like that about Americans who were fellow POWs/MIAs or their families? It is obscene. It is perfidy. The smiling image of Senator McCain that we see in the media is not the real John McCain. Who is the real John McCain? Perhaps one day we will learn who he is and why he has done what he has done to his fellow POWs. Perhaps.

The Senate Select Committee on POWs/MIAs swore to bring us the truth but, in the end, whitewashed it. The reason it was able to do that, in spite of the many testimonies of truth publicly given to the Committee, had to do primarily with the popularity and heroic stature among Americans of Senator John McCain. He was an American legend and was given a pass on whatever he did. It was assumed by the American public that Senator McCain would be the ideal person to sit on this Committee and would insist on the truth being told, since he himself had been a POW. He also brought a new look to politics. In his try for the 2004 presidency he openly spoke of his past indiscretions. This quality endeared him to the campaign press corps, all of who wanted tickets on his campaign bus tour, "The Straight Talk Express."

## MCCAIN'S FOLLIES

John McCain refused to co-sponsor:
- The 1984 Agent Orange Bill
- The 1992 Senate Select Committee on POW/MIA Affairs
- The 1996 Missing Persons Personnel Act
- The 1998 Persian Gulf Health Care Act
- The Bring Them Home Alive Bill

Thomas Birch, a Washington lawyer and National Chairman - National Vietnam Veterans Coalition, spoke of McCain: "When they held the hearings, it was McCain who handled the family members in a very rough manner, reducing one woman to tears. There are a lot of folks who compared him to Jane Fonda after he hugged Bui Tin, a former North Vietnamese army officer and interrogator/torturer of American prisoners of war, or POWs, who testified at the hearings." However, Jane Fonda was not a former POW in Vietnam and Jane Fonda was not a United States senator that had full access to documents that belied what he said in public. Birch noted that whenever one crosses McCain "he gets very ugly." Orson Swindle, former federal trade commissioner and former POW told Birch that McCain had threatened to destroy him because he supported George Bush in South Carolina. Beyond all this anecdotal information about John McCain, John Kerry or any other public figure, lies powerful testimony taken from the very Senate Select Committee on POW/MIA matters so dominated by these two senators. Read the following memorandum.

## THE INCREDIBLE McCREARY MEMORANDUM

Since about 700 POWs were cited in intelligence documents and even in a speech by a senior North Vietnamese general that was discovered in Soviet archives by an American scholar, why was it that at the end of its term the committee could have concluded that there is no viable evidence that more than a handful of POWs were still alive? The answer: Kerry hid the evidence and gave orders to have it shredded. The shredding ceased only when some staffers staged a protest and wrote memos calling for a criminal investigation. A memo provided by John F. McCreary, Defense Intelligence Analyst, lawyer and staff intelligence analyst states that the committee's chief counsel, J. William Codinha, a Kerry friend, "ridiculed the staff members" that protested such action. He said, "Who's the injured party?" Staffers replied, "The 2,494 families of the unaccounted-for U.S. servicemen." McCreary's memo contained startling allegations. The memo title was: *Memorandum for: Vice Chairman, Senate Select Committee on Prisoners of War and Missing in Action.* "Subject: Legal Misconduct and Possible Malpractice in the Select Committee." The following is a slightly reduced version of the memorandum:

1. As a member of the Virginia State Bar, I am
obliged by Disciplinary Rule DR-1-103(a) to report

knowledge of misconduct by an attorney "to a tribunal or other authority empowered to investigate or act upon such violations." Under Rule IV, Paragraph 13, of the Rules for the integration of the Virginia State Bar, this obligation follows me as a member of the Bar, regardless of the location of my employment, for as long as I remain a member of the Virginia State Bar. Therefore, I am obliged, as a matter of law and under pain of discipline by the Virginia State Bar, to report to you my knowledge of misconduct and possible prima facie malpractice by attorneys on the Select Committee in ordering the destruction of Staff documents containing Staff intelligence findings on 9 April 1992 and in statements in meetings on 15 and 16 April to justify the destruction.

2. The attached Memoranda for the Record, one by myself and another by Mr. Jon D. Holstine, describe the relevant facts, which I summarize herein:

a. On 9 April 1992, the Chairman of the Senate Select Committee, Senator John Kerry of Massachusetts, in response to a protest by other members of the Select Committee, told the Select Committee members that "all copies" would be destroyed. This statement was made in the presence of the undersigned and of the Staff Chief Counsel who offered no protest.

b. Later on 9 April 1992, the Staff Director, Frances Zwenig, an attorney, repeated and insured the execution of Senator Kerry's order for the destruction of the Staff intelligence briefing text. I personally delivered to Mr. Barry Valentine, the Security Manager for SRB-78, the original printed version of the intelligence briefing text. I also verified that the original was destroyed by shredding in the Office of Senate Security on 10

April 1992, along with 14 copies.

c. On 15 April 1992, the Staff Chief Counsel, J. William Codinha of Massachusetts, when advised by members of the Staff about their concerns over the possible criminal consequences of destroying documents, minimized the significance of the act of destruction, ridiculed the Staff members for expressing their concerns; and replied, in response to questions about the potential consequences, "Who's the injured party?" and "How are they going to find out because it's classified?"

d. On 16 April, the Chairman of the Senate Select Committee, Senator John Kerry, stated that he gave the order to destroy "extraneous copies of the documents" and that no one objected. Moreover, he stated that the issue was "moot" because the original remained in the Office of Senate Security "all along."

3. The foregoing facts establish potentially a prima facie violation of criminal law and a pattern of violations of legal ethics by attorneys in acts of commission and omission.

a. . . . an attorney may not direct the commission of a crime. In this incident two attorneys, one by his own admission, ordered the destruction of documents, which could be a violation of criminal law.

b. Neither the Staff Chief Counsel nor any member of the Select Committee made a protest or uttered words of caution against the destruction of documents, by admission of the Chairman, Senator Kerry. The Chief Counsel has an affirmative duty to advise the Staff about the legality of its actions . . . .

c. The Chief Counsel's statements during the 15 April meeting to discuss the document destruction showed no regard for the legality of the action and displayed to the Staff only a concern about getting caught.

d. The Staff Director's action in placing an un-accounted-for copy of the intelligence briefing text in the Office of Senate Security on 16 April constitutes an act to cover-up the destruction. Throughout the 16 April meeting, all three attorneys persisted in stating that the document had been on file since 9 April. This is simply not true.

4. I believe that the foregoing facts establish a pattern of grave legal misconduct - possibly including orders to commit a crime, followed by acts to justify and then to cover up that crime. ... I am obliged to recommend that this report be filed with the appropriate disciplinary authorities of the State Bars in which these attorneys are members.

(Signed)
John F. McCreary, Esquire

And yet, here is what Kerry said on Jan 21, 1992: "I want people to understand, again, that the committee is not withholding information or deep-sixing anything. All of it will be made public." This scandalous, perhaps criminal, behavior indicates to the reader why this book has been written. We need to expose these men. Thousands of documents that, if declassified or properly used, would have assisted the nation in finding and retrieving our POWs/MIAs. Instead, they were put into deep freeze by our government. Many attempts to declassify them were met with stiff opposition by Senators McCain and Kerry. If the Chairperson of a Congressional Committee, in this case, John Kerry, commits possible crimes in destroying information designed to assist POW families in learning what has happened to their loved ones, and we the American people allow it to pass without demanding an investigation, we are in deep trouble. Kerry himself said at the beginning of the hearings, "[Intelligence service employees] are not permitted to deny information to this committee on the basis of that [secrecy] oath . . . we intend to put them under oath and depose them, and we will subpoena them if necessary." And look at this Kerry statement: "—but we do not want at the end of this process anybody who has legitimate information to feel that this committee was not receptive to it." Really? How hollow all of this sounds compared to the Committee's own Defense Intelligence analyst accusing John Kerry and others of committing "potentially a prima facie violation of criminal law and a pattern of violations of legal ethics by attorneys in acts of commission and omission." How dare Kerry then accuse emotionally charged, frustrated, and lied-to members of POW/MIA families of presenting "wild-eyed, cock-eyed theories." He should be ashamed of himself. When Kerry ran for President in 2004, a blurb on his web site read: "When John Kerry returned home from Vietnam, he joined his fellow veterans in vowing never to abandon future veterans of America's wars. Kerry's commitment to veterans has never wavered and stands strong to this day."

That Kerry could have been bold enough to make that statement in 2004, after having disgraced himself at the 1992 Hearings is simply amazing. Equally amazing, I suppose, is that we Americans could have accepted that statement after his dishonorable conduct during the Senate Select hearings. Our free press dropped the ball on this one. Here was a man, accused by a defense analyst on his own staff of possible criminal activity in destroying POW documents during the hearings, proudly trumpeting his POW credentials as a future president of the United States. We can accept, if for no other reason than to make sure we are being fair, that Kerry fought bravely during the Vietnam War; what we cannot accept, since there is an overabundance of evidence to the contrary, is that he acted honorably as the Chairman of the Senate Select Hearings on POW/MIA Issues.

Kerry also, in concert with John McCain, got the Senate to agree to the normalization of diplomatic relations with the Vietnamese even though they had not returned all our POWs. McCain should have his hearing and his sight checked. After hearing from generals and diplomats, intelligence experts and groups that issued such important documents as *The Tighe Re-*

*port*, he continued to say that he had seen no "credible" evidence that more than a tiny handful of men might have been alive in captivity after 1973. He dismisses a number of the subsequent radio intercepts, live sightings, satellite photos, CIA reports, defector information, recovered enemy documents, reports of ransom demands and information indicating live captives, as meaningless. He has even described these intelligence reports as the rough equivalent of UFO and alien sightings. He writes that as a result of some of the things he did while in captivity he was so ashamed of himself that he made two half-hearted attempts at suicide; that he lived in "dread" that his father would find out. "I still wince," he says, "when I recall wondering if my father had heard of my disgrace."

In Congress, where his fellow legislators, colleagues and staffers have seen him cut people down in both open and closed meetings, they just shake their heads, unable to understand where he is coming from and what demons chase him incessantly. Insisting upon anonymity so as not to invite one of his verbal assaults, they say they have no easy way to explain why a former POW would work so hard and so persistently to keep POW/MIA information from coming out.

How insensitive he was to the feelings of POW families that have hungered for years to know what happened to their loved ones. As Co-Chairman Senator Smith pointed out to his fellow-senators: "But the point is: the reason why the Committee is in existence, the reason why you are here, and the reason why the debate is still raging is because the American people do not believe that their government has told them the truth. . . ."

Carol Hrdlicka, wife of David Hrdlicka (POW/MIA), testified with simple eloquence on 12/03/92: "If these men are not alive today, it's because they were starved, executed, mistreated, or simply died of broken hearts in the last 20 years it has taken to go looking for them. They know where my husband is. I know this. My family will not rest until we find the fate of David."

But there were heroes in that Committee.

Senators Smith and Grassley will be remembered into eternity for being honest, for attempting to find the truth, for the pain they must have suffered when fellow-senators betrayed their vow to find the truth, thus betraying the nation. Obviously, with each passing day the number of our captured loved ones who remain alive dwindles but, even when all have died in captivity, we must expose those who knew but would not act.

## THE TRUTH BILL

In 1989, 11 members of the House of Representatives introduced a measure they called "The Truth Bill." A brief and simple document, it said: "[The] head of each department or agency which holds or receives any records and information, including live-sighting reports, which have been correlated or possibly correlated to United States personnel listed as prisoner of war or missing in action from World War II, the Korean conflict and the Vietnam conflict, shall make available to the public all such records and information held or received by that department or agency. In addition, the Department of Defense shall make available to the public, with its records and information, a complete listing of United States personnel classified as prisoner of war, missing in action, or killed in action (body not returned) from World War II, the Korean conflict, and the Vietnam conflict." The Truth Bill was bitterly opposed by the Pentagon, so it got nowhere. It was reintroduced in the next Congress in 1991, and met the same fate.

## THE McCAIN BILL

McCain had a surprise for those who wanted openness. Out of the Senate came a new piece of legislation called, "The McCain Bill." As he had been doing all along since being appointed to the Select Committee, McCain did more slashing, cutting out the most important parts of the Truth Bill. One clause of his Bill actually said the Pentagon was not obligated to inform the public when it received intelligence that Americans were alive in captivity. Now, anyone with common sense is going to say that such a piece of legislation could not possibly get passed in an American Congress. But, America's love affair with war hero McCain had clout, and it became law. Boiled down, McCain's legislation declares that the Defense Department is not obligated to tell the public about prisoners believed alive in captivity and what efforts are being made to rescue them. It only has to notify the White House and the intelligence committees in the Senate and House, and the committees are forbidden under law from releasing such information. The McCain Bill is still being used to deny access to other sorts of records. For instance, an APBnews.com Freedom of Information Act request for the records of a mutiny on merchant marine vessel in the 1970s was rejected by a Defense Department official who cited the McCain Bill. Similarly, requests for information about Americans missing in the Korean War and declared dead for the last 45 years have been denied by officials who reference the McCain statute.

It's quite possible that Nixon, when he accepted the peace treaty of Jan. 27, 1973, had the intention of negotiating the release of the remaining POWs later. But, when Congress refused to provide the $3 billion to $4 billion in proposed national development reparations that National Security Adviser Henry Kissinger suggested, the chances of return of the abandoned men began to unravel. Washington rejected what it described as ransom money. The White House took the easy way out. It simply declared, falsely, that there were no more POWs/MIAs left to recover. And, cooperating in the cover-up, Hanoi did not correct the false impression that all the prisoners had been returned. Quid pro quo. For Vietnam, they got what they wanted without returning more POWs, and Washington got what it wanted, escaping from the trap of a very unpopular war at a time when Watergate was sapping all the energies of the President and his handlers.

## McCAIN & KISSINGER

As the website *VietNamVote.net* pointed out, McCain allied himself with the Nixon Administration's manner of dealing with North Vietnam, as carried out by Henry Kissinger. The Mc-

Cain/Kissinger connection was well defined by McCain. Senator McCain, on 03/09/07 said "When I have a question about something that's going on in the world, I call Dr. Kissinger and he is able to connect the dots for me. It is easy to be an expert on one aspect of some international situation. He's one of the only people I've ever known who can connect the entire scenario for you in a way that you understand the completeness of the challenge."

Kissinger made a secret trip to China on June 22, 1972, three years before the fall of Vietnam on 04/30/1975. He met with the head of government, Zhou Enlai, in Beijing. Kissinger told Zhou Enlai that the United States would consider accepting a communist takeover of South Vietnam if it occurred after a withdrawal of American troops. " . . . If we can live with a communist government in China we ought to be able to accept it in Indochina." He added that the U.S. would look the other way once our troops left Vietnam, if the communists took over. Kissinger declared that the White House would accept the results of "historical change." After concluding the deal with the North Vietnamese in 1972, Kissinger flew to Saigon to tell President Thieu that the presence of communist soldiers on South Vietnam soil would likely be part of any pact made. Thieu expressed his reaction: "Suddenly, I realized that things were being negotiated for us behind my back and without my approval." McCain has no problem with the behind-the-back deals made with China by the Nixon administration to sell out South Vietnam.

In an article entitled *Henry K takes Heat on MIAs*, *The New York Daily News* of Friday, June 22nd 2007 commented on Henry Kissinger's absence from the United States during the visit of Vietnam's President Nguyen Minh Triet to the United States. "A White House spokesman confirms to us that "a high U.S. priority" during the historic Oval Office summit would be "accounting for Americans still missing since the war."

Kissinger was playing a different tune than President Bush, when he said that he had no interest in revisiting the subject. Watergate had such a debilitating effect on Nixon that he scurried to get the POW Issue off the front pages, thereby halting whatever efforts had been in the making, including the 4.7 billion dollars promised to North Vietnam for the release of the remaining 700 POWs. Former Congressman John LeBoutillier is quoted by the *Daily News* as having written to Kissinger: "Hundreds of U.S. pilots and servicemen remain alive in captivity in captivity . . . You need to address your mistakes - and the fact that the North Vietnamese 'took' you at Paris. . . . You are directly responsible for this tragedy. It is still not too late for you to help bring these men home." *The Daily News* quotes Congressman LeBoutillier as saying: "Of course the guy's not going to admit he got duped. He won a Nobel Prize for this. What a weasel!" The cover-up continues and truth remains a casualty of the failed presidency of Richard Nixon.

Beginning below, prior to each chapter in this book, we will print letters that Father Pat received while we were working on the book. These letters will remind us of the human toll of lying to the families of American servicemen.

## LETTER FROM JOYCE USSERY

> From: "Joyce Ussery"  <juss1@getgoin.net>
> To:  pajbascio@yahoo.com
> Subject: Referred by Danny Belcher . . .
> Date: Wed, 14 Mar 2007 21:10:47 -0500
>
> Father Bascio:
> Your name and email address were forwarded by Danny Belcher. He has helped occasionally to try and get answers on some of our document questions regarding our Vietnam casualty etc., and he wanted us to contact you with our information. He mentioned that you were writing a book on the difficulties POW/MIA families have had in obtaining documentation and the truth of their loved ones. He thought you might like to hear our family's story. We are not an official POW/MIA family, but the family of a purported "KIA" with real concerns.

We are the family of Sgt. Carl Ussery, USA, a Forward Observer and Recon Sergeant attached to HHC 1/5 Cav and A Co., 1/5 from HHS (sometimes listed as B Co.) 1/77 Artillery for most of his time in Vietnam, December 3, 1967 to September 28, 1968, the date he was reported as killed in a fiery helicopter crash in Quang Tri Province. You'll find his name on panel 42 West, line 37. Carl was my childhood sweetheart and first husband. Seven years after his reported death, I married his older brother, married for 30 plus years, and we have three grown children.

On October 3, 1968, I was notified by an Army Chaplain, with telegram, that Carl had been "Hostile Missing" for 5 days, or since 09/28/68, and that "Search is in progress." An Army officer returned later the next the next day to inform that Carl's status was changed from "Missing to Dead," that his remains had been recovered and positively identified at the time of the crash. The Ussery family and I noted inconsistencies in what we were told then, i.e. as to how many men were on the helicopter, location of the crash, the questionable missing status for 5 days that they wouldn't address then and have since denied, etc., but we couldn't obtain further info then and soon attributed those irregularities to the "fog of war."

After a 1993 out-of-the-blue and interesting visit from one of Carl's Ft. Sill and then Vietnam comrades after 25 years, we decided to FOIA for Carl's personnel file from NPRC, St. Louis. When received, we found the file contained some very questionable documents, i.e. one stating remains were not positively identified . . . various other ones listing his "MIA"—"Missing"—"Hostile Missing" status . . . even one stating "body not recovered" and appears to be an early PUNCH report

. . . yet the Army still claims Carl was never actually missing. We are aware of pending IDs . . . but all documents we have indicate that he was considered more than a PID missing at the time. Again, we never received any explanation as to why he was first reported as "Hostile Missing" . . . and not until five days after the incident.

Most puzzling and of concern, within the NPRC file, we received documents with evidence that records were being kept on Carl by GSA in the years after his reported death, on at least 3 occasions, 70 07 07, 72 10 06, and as late as 73 07 27. These seeming "cover sheets" list the dates, "batch and page" numbers and an AR 7 digit number, along with Carl's name and identification numbers, both SSN and RA. We have tried repeatedly, but have not been able to obtain the text of what is in this documentation. When we press for answers as to why we can't get it, we and that question are basically ignored.

Associated with those documents is also a notation of finding it necessary to lose the records "for good" a month after we had just asked for the names of the survivors of the crash in late 1970; the notation of how they can't tell me the records are lost, and how the records show up after GSA tells someone from HQDA (at the Forrestal Bldg in DC) that they have a "live case on Ussery" (in 1972). If, in all of your research for your book, you ever run across any other GSA records being kept on Vietnam personnel, we would appreciate knowing of it. When those records were shown to Stony Beach reps (one covered Laos, one covered Cambodia) in June 2002 while in Washington, they claimed to be totally baffled as to why GSA would have been keeping any documentation on military personnel during the Vietnam era. One of the gentleman I spoke with emailed later to tell me that he could not get anywhere in getting information regarding the GSA records and that he was told to turn it over to DPMO.

For 27 years, we had placed flowers on the grave, assuming things were pretty much as we had been told in 1968. We now know that is not the case. By early March of 1996, this family had found it necessary to have the grave disinterred. I'm sure you are aware that families would not, nor would they be allowed to, do this without a valid, credible reason. The relatively good set of dental remains and long bone for height measurement were sent by our county coroner to the now late Michael Charney, PhD, an anthropologist from Ft. Collins, Colorado, for his determination. He soon called to tell me that the dental remains from the grave "do not match whatsoever" the SF 603 dental enlistment charting for Carl (known to be correct). We also noticed the height was too short for Carl/not within the anthropological range for Carl's actual known height. Dr. Charney's told us that he felt we had legitimate recourse to request that the Army do mtDNA testing on the remains that we have . . . that either the dental charting was wrong (it is known to be correct) . . . or that those were not the remains of Carl Ussery. We then engaged in a lengthy battle to try and get approval for mtDNA testing, and of course the Army denied that request, too, even with Dr. Charney trying to help convince them. Now that Carl's dental charting does not match, the Army is trying to say that the dental charting for Carl is incorrect/not reliable. So they are now discrediting the very method that the mortuaries used . . . often their only available method of identification . . . . during the Vietnam

War . . . We have even had private mtDNA "testing" done on the remains, but that was another costly, incomplete and "contaminated" fiasco that is another story within itself. We do have burned remains, but we question that they were in a white phosphorus fire, as we had been told in 1968. We do know they are not Carl's. There are two USN men still missing from that same day (they died of burns in an in-port boat explosion). We have been trying to get CILHI/AFDIL to at least check those family references against the remains we have . . . so far, to no avail, but we will keep trying.

I was going to make this a short summary, but I see it has already become a chapter! My apologies for the lengthy ongoing of this, but believe me, this just covers a very scant outline of the questions and concerns this family has and our ongoing quest to obtain the truth of the fate of our soldiers. I have tried to keep this introduction focused on some of the main questioned documents and the remains misidentification. Danny B. just felt that you would like to hear about it. Should you be interested in seeing any of the documentation mentioned, I have saved most of them in email files and can send them via email.

Best Regards,
Joyce Ussery

# CHAPTER THREE

# PERFIDY

**THIS IS NOT A MYSTERY NOVEL.** In mystery novels, the answer to the question, "who did it" comes at the end of the book. This book will come right to the point. There is sufficient evidence in this chapter to prove that government officials, agencies and public servants, each in their own way and for their own reasons, engaged in a cover-up of their insufficient attention to the whereabouts of American POWs and MIAs and, even more devastating, hid and even destroyed information about them. This chapter merely sets the scene. Then, in the ensuing chapters we will systematically analyze the betrayal by public officials of our American fighting men, their families, and the nation that put its trust in them. Read the following heartbreakingly despicable document, the Brzezinski Memo.

## THE BRZEZINSKI MEMO

Let me begin with a very simple but deviously dramatic memorandum to Zbigniew Brzezinski, National Security Advisor to President Carter. The memorandum was written by Michel Oksenberg, a Brzezinski aide. He informs Brzezinski that the League of MIA Families, a leading POW/MIA group in the United States, requests an appointment with him to discuss POW/MIA matters, and advises him to turn down the request. Mr. Oksenberg then sets out his strategy for lying, beginning with his suggestion that he call Ann Griffiths, the head of the organization, on behalf of Brzezinski, telling her that it is Brzezinski's desire that Griffiths speak with him instead. He then goes further and advises him to pretend that both he and the president are seriously interested in the POW question. He reminds him (and this is really shocking beyond belief) that both the State Department and the Defense Intelligence Agency (the parent agency for the Department of POW/MIA Affairs) are cooperating in playing this game. Here are his own words, "This is simply good politics: DIA and State are playing this game, and you should not be the whistle blower." Incredibly, Oksenberg is advising the President's National Security Advisor to lie and pretend, to deceive the American people *just as the State Department and the Defense Intelligence Agency do.* We would have to put our heads in the sand not to clearly understand that the American people have been lied to for many years. We have been duped into believing that the government had an intense interest in finding and recovering our POWs while, in fact, the government was distancing itself from the entire Issue, wanted nothing to do with it and, for "reasons of state," secretly opposed continued attempts to find and recover our POWs.

## STATUTES OF LIMITATION

There is no political statute of limitation on exposing the Defense Intelligence Agency, and the State Department of that time. Mr. Oksenberg's memo is clear and unmistakable evidence of perfidy. There may also be no statute of limitation on prosecuting those involved in such a plan to deceive the public. The memo points to a betrayal of oaths of office and possible charges of malfeasance in the non-fulfillment of duties solemnly assigned, in matters of the highest and greatest urgency and importance to the United States of America. We are writing this book with the hope that a new inquiry, in the form of an Independent Inquiry, will be initiated by our government, headed by a man or woman of high moral stature in the nation, to expose and punish all who participated in these conspiracies to hide the truth. Let us start with the man who wrote that letter and take it from there. If a man can go to jail for stealing a loaf of bread, then most certainly a man who writes such a letter to the President's National Security Advisor should be punished. In this case, Michel Oksenberg conspired to deceive the American public and dishonor fighting men and their families in a most sensitive and vital area of national life. This is not an accusation we make; it is a self-accusation written in his words, and on public record. He and others that so conspired betrayed our nation and, therefore, regardless of their rank, party or station, need to be publicly exposed and punished. Until that happens, the betrayals, heartaches, abandonment and outright treachery, deceit and obfuscation on the part of public servants will never allow men of good will and loyalty to the United States of America to have confidence in the leadership of this great Republic. Here is Mr. Oksenberg's infamous and perfidious memorandum in all its ugliness:

### MEMORANDUM FOR:
### ZBIGNIEW BRZEZINSKI

**From:** MICHEL OKSENBERG

**Subject:** Renewed League of MIA Families request for Appointment

Once again, the National League of MIA Families of American Prisoners and Missing in Southeast Asia seeks to meet you (Tab B).

They have nothing new to say, and I am capable of summarizing any developments for you. So, I recommend turning down the request, and I will call Ann Griffiths separately to say you have instructed me to see her.

However, a letter from you is important to indicate that you take recent refugee reports of sightings of live Americans "seriously." This is simply good politics: DIA and State are playing this game, and you should not be the whistle blower. The idea is to say that the President is determined to pursue any lead concerning possible live MIAs.

Do not offer an opinion as to whether these leads are realistic. Apparently you revealed skepticism to Congressman Gilman, and my recom-

mended letter to the League walks you back from
that. Recommendation: That you sign the letter at
Tab A to Ann Griffiths.

Then, in April, 1979, National Security Advisor Brzezinski advised President Carter that: "The National League of Families remains convinced that live American POWs remain in Vietnam. They also believe you are not being adequately informed and that the bureaucracy is not pursuing the matter aggressively. This case has little merit." Brzezinski played the game. All the players in the game knew they were lying, but in this conspiratorial brotherhood lying was itself the game. When Marine Corps PFC Robert Garwood returned in 1979, an NSC staffer wrote: "It would be politically wise for the President to indicate his continued concerns with the MIAs . . . since the Administration had implied earlier that it believed Vietnamese assurances that there were no Americans left behind in Hanoi."

Brzezinski's concern was not for the POWS, but for the political fallout of National League of Families of American Prisoners and Missing in Southeast Asia concerns over the lack of action on the part of the Carter Administration. The same Michel Oksenberg who wrote that perfidious memo testified before the Senate Select Committee 06/25/92 and had this to say about a New Jersey serviceman and his family members who were asking the government to find and rescue him. "The government owed it to the New Jersey soldier and others like him, as well as to their families and friends, to persist in a search for them as long as a straw of hope of their survival existed and to recover their remains if all hope had vanished." He was not going to blow the whistle on his office, and those of the State Department, the Department of Defense and the Defense Intelligence Agency!

And the same Anne Griffiths referred to in the above document appealed the decision of the DIA not to release documents. She wrote to Rear Admiral Curwhalter, Acting Director of the DIA.

This was his reply:

> Dear Ms Griffiths:
> This is in response to your letter of 22 March 1982, in which you appeal DIA's decision not to release live sighting reports of U.S. personnel in Southeast Asia received after 1 August 1979. . . .
> It is the policy of this Agency that all live sighting reports of U.S. personnel in Southeast Asia received after 1 August 1979 are properly classified in their entirety and are exempt from release under provisions of 5 U.S.C. 552 (b) (1), Freedom of Information Act. . . . Thus, release of the information in the form you requested would be counterproductive to our intelligence efforts in this vital area. Your appeal for release of these documents is therefore denied.
>
> Sincerely,
> E. A. Curwhalter, Jr.
> Rear Admiral, USN

That live sightings received after 1 August 1979 cannot be released is a slap in the face to the POW/MIA men and their families, keeping them in the dark after years of painful anxiety. It is cruel and unworthy of a government official no matter his rank, name or political affiliation.

The Select Committee's bipartisan, unanimous report was issued on January 13, 1993. Shortly after that, Clinton became President. Later that year McCain and Kerry made a visit to Vietnam. In what turned out to be a watershed meeting at the White House on June 11, 1993, less than two weeks after their visit to Hoa Lo prison, where McCain spent some time imprisoned, McCain and Kerry urged the President to lift the embargo.

They offered a variety of geopolitical and economic reasons, arguing that the Vietnamese had fulfilled all the promises they had made relative to the POWs/MIAs, so we should now lift the embargo.

Of course, both senators knew full well that there was a superabundance of testimony at their hearings that proved beyond a reasonable doubt that there were dozens and dozens and dozens of American POWs waiting, hoping and praying that our government would put pressure on the Vietnamese to release them. That never happened. These senators at that White House meeting betrayed our missing servicemen and their families, were less than candid with the president, and besmirched the honor of our nation. On another occasion, on June 19th, President Clinton went to Boston to deliver the commencement address at Northeastern University. Senator Kennedy accompanied him. At that event, John McCain got the President aside and did his best to convince him that normalizing relations with Vietnam was the right thing to do for a host of reasons important to the United States. Clinton did not move in that direction until later that fall. In January, 1994, a Kerry-McCain-sponsored Senate resolution urged the President to lift the embargo. Veteran groups did protest, but McCain remained a POW icon in America and when the vote came up it passed sixty-two to thirty-eight. McCain was delighted. "The vote will give the President the kind of political cover he needs to lift the embargo."

Senator Bob Smith, who was vice-chair of Kerry's committee, urged Clinton "not to be deceived," and argued against lifting the embargo, our only bargaining chip in our search for the POWs. In the end, on February 4, 1994, President Clinton did lift the embargo, and the Vietnamese negotiators, who certainly had not gone to Harvard, must have laughed up their collective sleeves at how easy it was for them to get something for nothing from the pinstriped, well groomed and rich Americans. Senators Dole and Phil Graham of Texas introduced a bill urging Clinton not to grant full diplomatic recognition to Vietnam until the United States first urged and was satisfied with North Korean progress in providing us access to full knowledge of the whereabouts and condition of 1,619 missing Americans.

Fearful of the possibility that Clinton might be persuaded by senators Dole and Graham, on May 23, 1995, Kerry and McCain met with Clinton in the Oval Office, once again making the case for having diplomatic relations, against the arguments that Dole had presented.

Against Dole, they made the case for normalization.

McCain was dramatic: "It doesn't matter to me anymore, Mr. President, who was for the war and who was against the war. I'm tired of looking back in anger." Clinton was impressed, and on July 11, 1995 he invited government, military, congressional and veterans group leaders to the White House and told them, "Today I am announcing the normalization of diplomatic relationships with Vietnam." *The New York Times*, on February 4, 1994, carried the headline, "Clinton Drops Trade Embargo on Vietnam," along with that famous photograph of a naked girl running toward the camera.

The extent to which the Nixon Administration was eager to sign a peace treaty with Vietnam is reflected in an article, Exchange of Prisoners in 1973, written by Vietnamese General Tran Van Tra, in charge of the proposed exchange of prisoners. He speaks of Ambassador Woodward and how helpful he was. Tran Van Tra kept hinted that he was going to hand over POWs just to get what he wanted while playing games with the Americans. Woodward, he wrote, offered him the use of a U.S. plane, which he accepted. "Woodward was openly very pleased, thanked me profusely and, in order to express his gratitude, inquired about my health and asked if I had any plans for the future. I replied that I planned to take a trip to Hanoi and, along the way, visit Laos. Woodward and Wickham thought that I intended to help resolve the question of American and puppet POWs in Laos . . . Woodward appeared to be very anxious and asked, 'When do you plan to go?' 'I'll go tomorrow if you'll provide the means.' He replied, 'You will have the means. I'll arrange for a C130 flight to Hanoi tomorrow morning.' "

Tran Van Tra then comments that he continued to play games with the Americans, who were taking him seriously. He told Ambassador Woodward that he would like to stop off at Paris on the way to Hanoi, and Woodward took him seriously. "Woodward was very pleased, said that that was a good idea, and said goodbye. He did not forget to affirm that an airplane would be available on the following morning. On the morning of 30 [March] 1973 the puppet officer who brought a convoy of sedans to pick me up at my residence and take me to the ramp of the airplane was very deferential." He was enjoying this fantasy game with the Americans, calling them puppets, and laughed up his sleeve at their naiveté.

## THE WATERGATE FACTOR

Nixon's preoccupation with Watergate was clearly seen by those working with him as having weakened and distracted him to the point that his ability to think through the many complications of recognizing Vietnam was severely compromised. While Nixon's handlers were busily using secrecy as a way of doing Watergate damage control, they were at the same time preoccupied with keeping secret information that related to our POWS. They wanted out of Vietnam at any cost, including the cost of abandoning our servicemen. The Watergate fiasco became the trigger for the Paris Peace Accord disaster. A member of Kissinger's National Security Council staff, Peter Rodman, testified before the Select Committee:

"I think knowing all the risks that we were heading into as 1973 began, none of us anticipated Watergate and how it would explode and totally wipe out Nixon's political leverage." We were weakened internally to such an extent that our demands of the North Vietnamese were immediately and robustly countered by immediate and robust rejections by them. Watergate had made us a paper tiger. The great United States of America became a helpless giant that surrendered as diplomatically as it could, leaving other POW issues unresolved and our men trapped in Vietnam, caught in the crossfire of government neglect and incompetence. The Watergate scandal stymied the Nixon administration. Henry Kissinger, 09/22/92, testified to the Senate Select Committee as gently as he could.

". . . it is quite possible that President Nixon did not have the same strength to resist that pressure as he might have had without Watergate. He never said that to me."

Rodman testified on 09/21/92 that the analysis made at that time was that "some of the crucial votes in the Congress that we used to defeat were lost this time and it was probably because of the demoralization of the President's supporters, so this was an unanticipated factor . . . .What I think happened was we evolved through the Watergate era on this issue, and it just dragged on and on . . . And to our discredit, I think, it (the POW Issue) kind of left the consciousness of nearly everyone. But I think those of us who knew the truth . . . were always bothered by this. I don't know what else I can say."

You can see the apology of Rodman looming large over his personality, as he regrets to admit that Watergate helped closed the gate to an honorable settlement of the Vietnam War issues, especially those concerning our POWs/MIAs. His testimony gives witness to his sorrow that that is the way it all turned out. As wrenching as it was to his internal psyche, he told the truth and liberated himself from the ghost that followed him. Whatever value there is in all of this, the cruel truth remains that our POW/MIAs remained forgotten and ignored as we shuffled the Paris Peace Accord diplomatic documents. That fact is a mark of shame on this nation, perpetrated not by foreign agents, but by men, honored and admired, who worked in the offices of the United States government, men whose patriotism it would have been almost impossible for fellow-Americans to question.

In 1994, the United States ranked fourteenth among foreign investors in Vietnam. About a year later it ranked sixth. McCain and Kerry take pride in that accomplishment. That's fine, but where are our POWs, what condition is Vietnam in today, what brutality is carried out in the dark corridors of its prisons and detention centers? Millions of people have paid a high price so that John McCain and John Kerry could claim victory in their struggle to restore diplomatic relations with Vietnam. We had the opportunity to be honorable in the Paris Peace Accords, but we blew it. What we had to do, i.e., as Senator Dole constantly reminded us at that time, was hold the signing of the peace documents until the Vietnamese provided us with a genuine list of names of those whom they had in custody. Unfortunately, the further we got away from the Nixon declaration that all our men were home, the more the POWs lost their bargaining value to

Hanoi, and ransom dollars never materialized. However, one item did, at least temporarily, throw our diplomats into confusion. It was a top-secret Soviet intelligence document containing a report to the Hanoi politburo by a senior North Vietnamese general. A Harvard researcher, Stephen Morris, uncovered it. The report was dated in September 1972, just four months before the signing of the peace accords. If that report, entitled: "1,205 American Prisoners," had been available to the American press at the time of Nixon's famous declaration that all our POWs had been returned home, he would probably have had to leave office in disgrace. The report read: "1,205 American prisoners of war [are] located in the prisons of North Vietnam—this is a big number. Officially, until now, we published a list of only 368 prisoners of war [the number Hanoi was then admitting at the Paris talks]. The rest we have not revealed. The government of the U.S.A. knows this well, but it does not know the exact number of prisoners of war and can only make guesses based on its losses. That is why we are keeping the number of prisoners of war secret, in accordance with the [Hanoi] politburo's instructions."

Predictably, Vietnam, after two decades of publicly denying it had held back any prisoners, angrily called the document a fabrication. Washington, too, became apoplectic. Though forced to acknowledge that the report was an authentic Soviet document, the Pentagon nonetheless insisted that it "is replete with errors, omissions, and propaganda that seriously damage its credibility." Specifically, the Pentagon said the 1,205 figure had to be in error because this would mean that 600 additional POWs existed and such a conclusion was "inconsistent with our own accounting." That was not the truth. After all, when Hanoi released the 591 men in 1973, the Pentagon itself said there were still 1,328 Americans missing in action and unaccounted for. If half or less were alive, the 1,205-prisoner document would hardly be "inconsistent with our own accounting."

The Paris Peace Accords, as crafted by Kissinger, provided that prisoner lists would be exchanged the day that the agreement was signed, and all prisoners of war would be returned within 60 days. But, when we received the list of U.S. prisoners, on that list were missing more names than it contained. We had been betrayed by an enemy we should not have trusted in the first place. Of course that was hidden under a bushel as our business community rushed into Vietnam like the California gold rush experience. Ironically, it took the Communist Pathet Lao to tell us that Vietnam held many more of our military, especially American pilots. This, in spite of the fact that since they were not invited to participate in the Parish Peace Accords they were not bound by it. They even offered to meet one-on-one with us. This offer was totally ignored by our government, in spite of the fact that Laos has an embassy not too far from the White House.

President Nixon did protest to the Vietnamese Prime Minister complaining that their list contained only ten POWs from Laos (one of whom was a Canadian) while our records showed that 317 Americans were unaccounted for in Laos. But, he had already signed the Peace Accord and he had already ordered our troops to begin returning home. It was too late.

There were some last-minute threats of American military options emanating from the Department of Defense but, in the end, Nixon caved in.

The Administration quickly went into high gear to paint a picture that would convince the American people that the United States had won. But, during the Senate Select committee hearings, Kissinger pointed out the Senate's rejection on May 31, 1973 of an amendment offered by U.S. Sen. Robert Dole that called for the bombing of North Vietnam, Laos and Cambodia if North Vietnam. However, the Select Committee did note that "some Administration statements at the time the agreement was signed expressed greater certainty about the completeness of the POW return than they should have. . . ."

The Committee was giving with the right hand but taking away with the left hand. While admitting that the Nixon Administration did not do as good a job as it should have, they capsu lated the Nixon failure with the mantra that "The Administration may have raised expectations too high."

That mantra was a cover-up because it implies that the only thing the Administration did wrong was raise expectations too high. The truth is that they purposely and deliberately lowered expectations as much as they possibly could so that their failure to do enough, their failure to hold North Vietnamese feet to the fire would go unnoticed. In plain language, they lied like hell.

## EMBARGO AND DIPLOMATIC RELATIONS

All major U.S. veteran organizations, the two POW/MIA family groups, and the majority of Vietnamese Americans in this country opposed President Clinton's lifting of the Vietnam embargo. Clinton's predecessor, George Bush, who during the 1992 Presidential campaign was booed at a convention of POW/MIA activists, wisely left it to Clinton to make that decision. It was a political hot potato. Of course the Kerry/McCain unity on this Issue gave it an appearance of bi-partisanship. That Kerry was eager to have the embargo lifted is attested to by the fact that he traveled to Vietnam eight times, and spent a good deal of time during the Senate Select Committee hearings moving in and out of this subject. McCain and Kerry lobbied very hard to dissipate the atmosphere in the nation that no lifting of the Vietnam embargo should take place unless and until Vietnam returned our POWs. Therefore, McCain and Kerry had to find a wedge that would discount this national sentiment. Here was the wedge. The Senate Select Committee in Its final report concluded that:

". . . while the Committee has some evidence suggesting the possibility a POW may have survived to the present, and while some information remains yet to be investigated, there is, at this time, no compelling evidence that proves that any American remains alive in captivity in Southeast Asia."

Now of course there were many discussions that took place on this subject among POW/MIA families and, naturally, not everyone thought exactly the same, but on one issue all were in agreement: No ending of the embargo and no diplomatic recognition of the Hanoi regime until and unless they came clean on our POWs/MIAs. And so, it was at this point that John McCain became the POW families' principal adversary, the focus of their anger and frustration. John Kerry was his stoutest defender.

## COLONEL CORSO

Among those testifying was retired Colonel Phillip Corso (US Army Ret.), now deceased. Corso was a former National Security Aide and POW specialist to President Eisenhower. He was present during the exchange of prisoners at Panmunjom in Korea at the end of the war. Incredibly, his previous attempts to tell our government what happened to Americans there were ignored. Following the Korean War, Col. Corso was on Eisenhower's White House staff, in charge of the POW Issue. In Senate and House hearings in 1992 and 1996, he explained how Eisenhower made the decision to leave the missing American POWs behind after he, Corso, had explained to Eisenhower that thousands were missing, that U.S. intelligence knew that hundreds had been shipped to Russia and China, and that achieving their return would be difficult. U.S. policy was clear, Corso explained: "We couldn't put pressure on the Soviet Union or the satellites, we couldn't. They had our prisoners and we couldn't put pressure on them. That was it. Our policy forbids us from doing it. If you did it, you were disobeying national policy."

In implementing this policy, U.S. executive agencies—State, intelligence, and Defense—subsequently denied any American POWs were left behind. Corso told the Committee that he knew of two train loads of U.S. POWs   containing about 450 prisoners, for a total of 900, heading for the Soviet Union, and that there might have been a third train. Corso also testified that he had received from two to three hundred reports on these 900 POWs and was asked to brief President Eisenhower personally on the situation. In a five-minute meeting which took place in mid-1953 or early 1954. "I had a call from my principal, C. D. Jackson, one day, who was special assistant to the President. He said, 'get over here; we have to go see the President. Bring your prisoner of war report.' My prisoner of war report that I handed him was one page. I walked in the office. The President was in the Oval Office, the three of us, and he said, 'I understand you have a report on prisoners of war going to the Soviet Union?' I told him, yes, that's what I'm here for."

Corso's report contained the estimate that at least 900, possibly up to 1,200 American POWs were involved. "I handed [President Eisenhower] the report, and he read it. And he had a very serious look on his face. . . . This was not a pleasant meeting. It did not last long. . . . He said, 'Colonel, do you have any recommendations, because in the military, generally the writer of the report has to make a recommendation to his superior who then decides on what to do with it?'

I said, "yes." Corso explained that once prisoners got into the hands of the KGB it is likely they would never return. "And I told him, 'Mr. President, you are aware of the system of the KGB, how they use prisoners of war and defectors?' And he said, 'Yes, I am.' He then said, 'Is your recommendation not to make it public?' I said, my recommendation is not to make public the part—the KGB operation . . . So, the President said, 'well, I accept your recommendation . . . I agree we cannot give it to the families.'

Then I said, "Mr. President, though, may I send a copy of this report to the Department of Defense?" He said, 'Yes.'"

Corso then explained to the Committee that it was the government's policy not to make strident and confrontational statements directed at the Soviet Union, North Korea and China. He testified that "The big policy was the policy of fear. Fear of general war. That was the policy that was stopping us."

Corso added that the families were not told because: "You'd have to tell the families that these boys were going to be tried, used, exploited for NKVD operations which were espionage, sabotage, and take their identities. And that we felt would have been damaging to the families, but it's hard to explain, sir. . . . They were going to be exploited in a very sinister way. As far as telling them they were alive, sir, I put in a speech at the United Nations that 1,800 prisoners of war had gone to the Soviet Union, had been transferred to the Soviet Union. Now, there was no mention that they were dead or not dead, but that was put in the statement and released, and he gave me permission to put that in."

Corso stated that five hundred of our POWs were not returned that the government knew were sick and wounded, and would not survive "unless they are brought back soon for treatment. As we had our staff meetings with the chief of staff and so forth I was briefed on the subject. I would brief my superiors on this and then the position was to compile this information in the form to send to Washington, to the Pentagon. Nothing was done in the Far East with this information." Corso also noted that when the information was sent back to Washington for processing or instructions, "generally, we never got any instructions back to do anything about it." Colonel Corso's story gets even darker as he spoke of his first-hand knowledge of many American military taken to the former Soviet Union, information he had personally shared with President Eisenhower.

## GOVERNOR WILLIAM CLEMENTS ON THE HOT SEAT

On May 22, 1973 acting Secretary of Defense William Clements received a routine POW memorandum from the DIA. concerning Americans unaccounted for after Operation Homecoming. The memorandum stated that: "Federal law provides the secretaries of the military services with exclusive authority to determine initially and later change the casualty classifications of personnel captured (POW), killed (KIA) or missing in action (MIA)." It then points to an exception: "The Military Services are not considering any status changes at this time. . . . However, one case involving an American civilian—Mr. Emmet Kay who was lost over Laos on 7 May 1973—is under review by the Department of State and this Agency for possible change of status from missing to captured."

Clements wrote at the bottom of that memorandum something which caught the eye of Senator Smith of the Senate Select Committee, since it signaled a departure from legally required procedures. "I want a memo sent to all departments (Services-ASD-DIA- JCS) etc. that any reclassification from MIA to POW must first be cleared by me. . . ."

The memo Clements ordered was prepared by Assistant Secretary of Defense Robert Hill and signed by Secretary Clements on June 8, 1973. It ordered the service secretaries to present to Clements for his personal review and approval all proposed status changes from MIA to POW. This is the memo:

*I request that all actions which recommend reclassification of military personnel from missing in action to captured status be submitted to me for approval. Proposed reclassification actions should be first routed through the Assistant Secretary of Defense for International Security Affairs for preliminary review before referral to me.*

In his deposition before the Senate Select Committee Clements revealed, however unconsciously, why it was he had arrogated that authority to himself. He was part of the government's desire to close discourse on POWs in an effort to speedily bring about a peace treaty with Vietnam. He admitted, at some point, that the service secretaries presented between 50 and 75 cases with a recommendation that a serviceman's status be changed from MIA to POW. He denied every request. And, when he appeared before the Select Committee on September 24, 1992 he claimed all status changes had been handled, not by him, but exclusively by the services throughout his tenure at DOD: Clements boldly lied. "In other words, the Navy classified their people, Army did theirs, and the Air Force did theirs . . . . want to make that very clear because it's important that your committee and the public at large understand that the office of the Secretary of Defense and/or the State Department and/or the National Security Council, nor the President, had any control whatsoever over classification."

This false statement prompted Senator Smith to intervene. Clements was called to testify before the Select Committee:

> **Sen. Smith:** Why did you, Gov. Clements, make a decision to not allow your service secretaries, which as far as I know has never happened before and has not happened since—to not allow your service secretaries to upgrade an individual from an MIA category to a POW category? Why did you make that decision?
>
> **Governor Clements:** I don't think that I made such a decision.
>
> **Sen. Smith:** You did not make that decision. Is

that your statement?

**Governor Clements:** I have no recollection of making a decision of that kind. Let me tell you something, Senator, it is very, very clear that only classification can be changed within the service. And let's don't get that confused.

**Sen. Smith:** (reads text of June 8 memo aloud) That was June 8th, 1973.

**Governor Clements:** That's right.

**Sen. Smith:** With your signature.

**Governor Clements:** And there's nothing wrong with that. . . .

**Sen. Smith:** Governor, you directed the Secretaries to route it all through you on June 8th. And on July 17th, you wrote to the president of the United States and you said: "In my view, the status determination process, as established by law and experience, should be allowed to function as prescribed."

**Governor Clements:** I agree with that.

**Sen. Smith:** That is what you said to the President, but that is not what you said on June 8th to the service secretaries.

**Governor Clements:** I disagree completely.

**Sen. Smith:** Well, I am not going to argue with you, Governor. It is a part of the record.

**Governor Clements:** Well, you don't have to argue with me, just read it again. .

**Sen. Smith:** Governor, I have got it in your own handwriting. . . "I want a memo sent to all departments, services, ASD, DIA, JCS, that any reclassification from MIA to POW must first be cleared by me." That is what you said.

**Governor Clements:** I want to review

**Sen. Smith:** In your own handwriting.

**Governor Clements:** I want to review every one of them. That's exactly right. This was a very, very delicate issue.

Clements' tortuous reasoning and confusion of thoughts reflected the embarrassment of having read back to him material he had written but had denied a few moments earlier. He was caught by his own words. In effect, he testified against himself. There is other testimony to point to Clements playing with the truth. Read this exchange between Senator Kerry and Dr. Roger Shields, of the office of the Assistant Secretary (ISA). Shields headed up the overall Department of Defense coordination responsibility for all PW/MIA matters. In 1973, Shields told President Nixon:

> "Mr. President, we do have two missing for every man that comes home." President Nixon said, "Right," and then changed the subject. The very next day the State Department said that no American POWs remained in Vietnam. Shields testified before the Select Committee on 06/25/92 that the POW list provided by the North Vietnamese to representatives of the U.S. Government in Paris in January, 1973 as required by the Paris Peace Accords was incomplete. Also it did not include the names of those prisoners missing in Laos. Shields said: "After briefing those who returned, we knew also that the names of some men who may have died in captivity were also not on the lists." These remarks prompted Senator Kerry to question Roger Shields.
>
> **Chairman Kerry:** To say all prisoners had returned as the President announced on the 29th of March, a week before your press conference, was wrong. He knew it was wrong. Let me tell you why. You recall going to see Sec. of Defense William Clements in his office in early April, a week before your April conference, correct?
>
> **Shields:**[1] That's correct.
>
> **Chairman Kerry:** And you heard him tell you, all the American POWs are dead. And you

said to him, "You cannot say that."
**Shields:** That's correct.
**Chairman Kerry:** And he repeated to you,
"You did not hear me. They are all dead."
**Shields:** That's essentially correct.

Clements, the United States Secretary of Defense appears here to be telling Shields that even though the government had information that not all American POWs were dead, it was Shields' job to say that they were all dead. There is no other way to interpret that conversation.

And we have McCain in an exchange with Shields:

> **Sen. McCain:** How do you account for the President of the United States saying all POWs are home?
>
> **Dr. Shields:** Senator, I don't control the statements of the President of the United States. I did not at that time. I was as dismayed at that statement as anyone else was. . . .

That same day, in an exchange with Kerry, Shields said: "In the cases of Charles Dean and Neal Sharman, we knew that they had been captured. That was not a secret. We made that evidence available to anyone, and we acknowledged that. We did not bring them home. We were not able to do that." Shields is also put on the spot by Senator Smith. He tells Shields that based on the documents that he had read, the depositions the committee had taken, the witnesses they had talked to, it was a fact that the Secretary of Defense made a recommendation to resume the war and risk bringing home the last group of American POWs. "So my question to you is, after the President speaks and says all the POWs are home, you had a private meeting with the President of the United States and you come out of that meeting and you hold another press conference. And you say, in addition to what the President already said, that there are no more living Americans in Vietnam. . . . Did anybody say anything to you prior to that meeting, at any time, about what you should or should not say to the President of the United States, yes, or no?"

The answer was in the negative. Senator Smith later talks with General Major General Richard Secord. Laos Chief of Air Operations, Central Intelligence Agency, 1966-1968 and Laos Desk Officer, Defense Department, 1972-1975, asking why the government POW database looked differently when President Nixon made his statement:

> "What happened differently? Was there something there that we are missing that caused this change in analysis of the intelligence? Or do you believe that there were people there after Operation Homecoming, based on what you knew?"
>
> **General Secord:** "Well, yes, of course I believe there were people after Operation Homecoming."

Smith then tells Secord that it is his belief that two sets of books were kept; one for the Secretary of Defense, the real records:

"The only thing that changed is you guys made an announcement, or the President made an announcement on March 29th which was totally at odds with all of that data. I mean, there is just no way that any reasonable person can conclude based on the documents and the information that this committee has received, that you could make the kind of statement that the President made and know that it was correct. And I will tell you, to speak for myself; this one Senator just does not accept it."

Is there any spy movie you have seen that could match this real life James Bond scenario involving deception from the President down! Then, Robert Sungenis, Chief of the Directorate of Information, Operations and Reports, Office of the Secretary of Defense (1973-92), gave his testimony.

**Sungenis:** "The first casualty reporting requirement from the services was in 1963, and that was a numerical report only. In March of 1973 the requirement was made that the services provide us with individual casualty reports. And what they did in '73 was to provide us with a DD form 1300 for each individual and a punched card with that information. Since that day we have maintained the file. But as you know, this was after Homecoming when we got into the business."

Cooked books involving the President of the United States on a matter involving POWs, MIAs and their families? That could never happen, right? Wrong. Read this:

**Senator Smith:** "Actually, there were two policies, one right after the other, with the same database . . . the first policy was full accountability. Then there was a statement when the President said all the POWs are home. Wrong. The policy then changed to, everybody is home; all the POWs were home. But the database, the intelligence information that you had, did not support that claim, as you have all said."

So, Senators Smith, Grassley, Kerry and McCain themselves got answers from a very competent and strategically placed witness that what the President said was not telling the truth and that the Secretary of Defense Clements was not telling the truth. Now, try to figure out then why Kerry and McCain, heavily engaged in activity caricaturing Prisoner of War families as crazies, were hiding the truth that government officials, including the President, had lied, since their own public questioning of these same individuals proved that they were lying? If anything was ever a puzzle wrapped in a mystery this is one.

As of 1992 there were 1,278 military personnel who are unaccounted for as a result of the hostilities in Southeast Asia. Of this number, 67 were officially listed as prisoner of war. Clements gave this information to President Nixon on or about the 17th of July, 1973, and they were listed as "Current captured."

Obviously this conflicts with both the Nixon statement on March the 29th and the Shields statement on April 14th.

As Senator Grassley pointed out during the Committee hearings the listed prisoners thought to be alive on March 31, 1973 were 81; on 7 April, 1973, 80; on April 14, 1973, and that is the date that Shields made his statement that none were alive. As you can see, our civil servants responsible for accounting for the condition of our POWs and MIAs, either boldly lied to us, or were totally incompetent and confused.

## SOVIET INVOLVEMENT

On January 21, 1992, a Russian General, Kalugin, testified before the Senate Select Committee. The Committee was interested in finding out whether or not the Soviets held or interrogated American Prisoners of War either in Russia or elsewhere. It was a subject on which very few people had any knowledge. Because of Kalugin's testimony the veil of secrecy that hung over the subject was set-aside by the CIA, the KGB, and even Vietnam, each of which admitted that at least one American POW was interrogated by the Soviets. The American public had been told just the opposite. General Vessey testified before the Committee on 06/25/92 that a Colonel Nechiporenko, who was Kalugin's source, told Kalugin that he had interviewed one American in 1973, and the Vietnamese agreed that that was the case. The Russians were very interested in getting as much technical information from our American military as they could get. The Colonel later denied he had said any such thing, so General Kalugin was asked, "can you help us to understand why Mr. Nechiporenko allegedly said one thing to you at one moment and straight-out denies that he talked to anybody subsequently? Do you have an explanation for that?"

**General Kalugin:** "I think that's a premeditated lie on the part of the former intelligence organization, and I know the reason. . . . Vietnam remains one of the last listening posts in the Far East, and to lose a relationship with them . . . would probably be a major setback for the Soviet intelligence, so why not keep a story which was coordinated with the Vietnamese"

Kalugin also pointed out that the reason the Americans were interrogated in Vietnam, not the USSR was because Brezhnev feared that bringing an American prisoner to the Soviet Union would damage Soviet/American relations. "It makes no practical sense, no political or military sense . . . . I am sure that [Soviet military interrogation of U.S. POWs] happened, because they did have a major interest in American know-how in weaponry, details, and instructions."

Senator Reid asked Kalugin why the Committee should believe him since his official job required him to do a lot of lying for the Soviet Union.

General Kalugin: Well, it makes no sense. I am 57 and I've lived a very interesting life. Today I want to live a different life, just an honest and simple [one]. You may believe it—as I say, take it or leave it."

Senator Herb Kohl, of Wisconsin, on 11/15/91, made a really interesting point during his testimony, i.e., that it is the nature of man to learn from the past or to uncover parts of the past that as yet had not been made clear. "We even go as far back as a couple of thousand years and have an intense interest as to exactly where Christ was buried. Why then, should it be a problem for some senators and congressmen and folks in the executive branch to go back 40 years and find out what happened to American fighting men being abused and used as slave labor in Vietnam, or Laos or the Soviet Union? We inquired about many, many people in the Soviet Union about whom we were concerned—Soviet Jews, Muslims in the Soviet Asian Republics, the civil rights of Soviet writers, musicians, politicians, students, women, etc, etc, etc. Why are we not as intensely curious about our POWs who may yet be alive, for whose families it is a national honor and duty to account for? You tell me because I certainly do not know."

The Committee went through at least 3,000 reports and hundreds of thousands of hard copy documents. Tracking POWs was considered a national priority. An NSA employee, Jerry Mooney, testified before the Committee in 1992 that it is an "intelligence given. . . . The Soviets do take our people. . . ."

In their case, the Russians were not looking for slave labor; they wanted facts, lots of technological facts, so they would naturally deal with their friends and allies the North Vietnamese and tell them they wanted so and so to help understand such and such a machine or plane or whatever. This is common sense. If we were way behind the Soviets in technology we would do the same. Anyone who cannot see that is not intelligent enough to be a member of Congress or of the executive branch of government. Anyone who does not see that is walking on Cloud Nine. But, the Committee felt that there was not enough hard evidence to confirm Mooney's statements!

## TESTIMONY OF COLONEL DELK SIMPSON

The testimony of Col. Delk Simpson (USAF-Ret.), former U.S. military attaché in Hong Kong, generally agreed with the testimony of Col. Corso relevant to the fact that large numbers of U.S. prisoners were transferred to Soviet territory during the Korean War period. His information was that about 700 American prisoners, some of whom were black, were transported from Manchou-li, China into Siberia. Col. Simpson testified that when he tried on many occasions to bring this information to offices in both the executive and legislative branch he learned that DIA considered him to be "senile" and that the prisoners he had reported were French from the French-Indochinese War, being taken to Siberia for return to France. Later, Col. Simpson learned the likely reason why he had received such official inaction. At a meeting with Colonel Corso, he was told by Corso that from 1953 he, Corso, was the author of a policy while on the White House staff to abandon all prisoners being held by the Russians. He said the policy was approved by President Eisenhower. "Senator, it is incomprehensible to me that anybody would make such a decision to send our boys to a sure death."

## TESTIMONY OF MONIKA JENSON-STEVENSON

On November 7, 1991 Monika Jenson-Stevenson testified before the Senate Select Committee. She and her husband had spent the previous six years researching and writing a book on the POW/MIA Issue. She told the Senators that the public was hungry, even desperate, to find just "one segment of the U.S. Government that would champion the right to know the truth about what happened to American soldiers who were taken prisoner in a war that everyone wanted to forget about as soon as it was over." She pointed out that the POW/MIA Issue was a good starting point of the trust that either exists or should exist between the American people and the U.S. government on the important matter of the lives and welfare of the soldiers who risked life and limb to defend the nation. "Sadly, in my view, that trust has been badly abused by the government agencies that have controlled the Prisoners of War Issue." She pointed out, for example, that our missing servicemen in Laos were protected by no National Security umbrella. "They were simply designated nonexistent." She characterized the government position that there was no credible evidence of prisoners left behind in Laos or anywhere else in Southeast Asia as "a blatant lie, yet it is policy. We came across large amounts of credible evidence." She explained that she provided the evidence collected by the most expensive and the best technology in the world, as well as that reported by competent and loyal human agents, many of whom were our former allies and risked their lives and their limbs in that conflict, evidence that was described on her *60 Minutes* segment by General Tighe, as a miracle. "Now if the head of the Defense Intelligence Agency, in all those critical years knew that it was a miracle, we believe that the Interagency Group controlling the Prisoners of War also knew it. Yet almost all of the evidence, a lot of it has been inexcusably retired, left to disintegrate and be destroyed."

She also characterized the government's position that the Vietnamese have never offered to return prisoners as a lie. " . . . We have talked with people who were direct witnesses to meetings where the Vietnamese made a direct offer of prisoners for money. One was made to the Woodcock Commission in the late 70's . . . .The truth is that lies have become U.S. Government policy on prisoners." One of her sources was a retired high-ranking CIA man who personally saw prisoners in Laos in the early 80's. He not only reported this to the government but also was even able to name them. In the course of this exchange with the government the CIA man discovered that there was a deliberate organized attempt by some intelligence officials to misinform and harass the most active families of the missing. When the former CIA man asked the Justice Department for the full file he was told that the matter would have to be taken up with another government department and later, the official withheld the complete file because of a third agency's objection. What kind of justice is meted out by the Justice Department?"

## LAIRD, RICHARDSON AND SCHLESINGER

Testifying before the same Committee, Secretary of Defense Laird was asked why, when President Nixon declared that all POWs were now accounted for, even though people in his administration knew that they had not all returned home, why no one did anything about it. No one raised the issue, apparently, inside the Government after the President made his assertion in March of 1973. This was the exchange:

> "All I am asking—and I do not mean it to be in any way an accusatory question. I just would like you to describe the atmosphere that apparently permeated the White House and the administration in June when you arrived, re-arrived, about this issue? Why was it such that no one chose to challenge the president's statement and recharacterize it in a way that would be less positive, as you described it?"
>
> **Laird:** I cannot explain that, Senator. I believe that that's something you should pursue."

Schlesinger told the Senate Select Committee: "I can come to no other conclusion. . . . [S]ome were left behind." The intelligence and a flood of data since unearthed shows that the number was in the hundreds. When he testified he was asked why Nixon would have accepted this. He replied, "One must assume that we had concluded that the bargaining position of the United States . . . was quite weak. We were anxious to get our troops out and we were not going to roil the waters."

Then he was asked a very simple question: "In your view, did we leave men behind?"

"Some were left behind."

"I think that, as of now," replied the former defense secretary and CIA chief, "that I can come to no other conclusion, senator. . . . Some were left behind." The Schlesinger-Laird testimony was explosive, but merited a mere one-day mention in the media.

The thousands of reporters around the nation missed the obvious implications of this testimony.

I have looked high and low and have found no evidence that the testimony of these eminent men has been contradicted. On the contrary, let us do a bit of calculation. At the time of the Senate Select Committee hearings there were 1,278 military personnel who were unaccounted for as a result of the hostilities in Southeast Asia. Of this number, only 67 were officially listed as prisoner of war. That was the information from acting Secretary of Defense William Clements to President Nixon. And that is on, I believe, the 17th of July 1973. That means that we had a lot of work to do in determining how many of that large number of 1,211 could have been alive in custody, etc. So, although it might never have been possible to get the figure with 100 percent certitude, we would certainly have had to presume that they were, absent any proof to the contrary, in custody. In fact, in those days we had a category titled "Current captured." Therefore, President Nixon's statement on March 29th of that year that all our prisoners were accounted for was incorrect. The only previous study that was comparable in its original mandate to that of the Senate Select Committee was that of the Montgomery Committee in 1975-1976.

## MRS. DONNIE COLLINS

One woman, the wife of POW Captain Tom Collins (captured in October, 1965), testified before the Senate Select Committee on Dec 3, 1992, and told the senators what it is like to live one's life trying to discover the whereabouts of a POW. . . . [Y]ou become obsessed. You cannot sleep, eat, and work, because you would waltz with the devil to bring one man home." Senator Smith asked her if she ever saw or heard of any live-sighting reports on her husband. " I saw some in 1991. I was sent them from Hawaii." The senator informs her that he was aware of a live-sighting report that was available during the war. "If your husband was the subject of a live-sighting report, you should have been told that, and you were not. . . ."

Mrs. Collins' uncertainty about events that the government was fully aware of was precisely the problem that the Committee was tasked to clear up. "I, as an MIA wife, was frustrated by knowing little, being left out of the loop, and it seemed at times being treated as the enemy, more feared by the administration and military intelligence than the North Vietnamese whom we should have been unified against."

Even though the wives knew they were being fed a steady diet of lies by our government, they were very cautious of denouncing the government on the grounds that the government was engaged in war and they would be accused of dishonoring their POW loved ones. At the same time they suffered the painful indignity of being lied to and patronized by their own government. In one of the Committee hearings, Sen. Smith asked Mrs. Collins if she had ever heard of a report of a live-sighting of her husband Mrs. Collins replied, "Never, but I know that there are some now."

The senator confirmed that such a sighting of her husband had been reported, and that her husband had been captured in Laos by North Vietnamese regulars. And then there was this heart-rending exchange:

> **Vice Chairman Smith:** Do you have any reason to believe that anybody in the U.S.government knew he was alive and did not tell you?
>
> **Collins:** Oh, yes, I'm certain that they did. See, here we come back to the beginning.
>
> **Vice Chairman Smith:** So people in the United States government knew your husband was alive and they did not tell you.
>
> **Collins:** Yes.

## THE OSTRICH SYNDROME

A newcomer to this subject matter might reasonably ask why there is no great public outrage, no sustained headlines, no national demand for investigations, no penalties imposed on those who had hidden, and are still hiding the truth. One reason is that the press suffered from the ostrich syndrome; no major media organization ever carried out an in-depth investigation by a reporting team into the prisoner issue. When prisoner stories did get into the press, they would have a one-day life span, never to be followed up on. Thousands of Americans have demonstrated, signed petitions, appeared on talk shows, petitioned their senators and congressmen, but the truth never came out. However, it is not too late.

## CLASS ACTION SUIT AGAINST PRESIDENT REAGAN

The brave men who were tasked with finding our missing servicemen, men like Major Mark Smith and Sergeant First Class Melvin McIntire knew that there were 800 POWs at least and about 500 wounded service personnel within 5 miles of Panmunjom. Smith and McIntire had been assigned to a top-secret mission in Thailand to gather intelligence on whether U.S. POWs remained in Southeast Asia. At some point in time they realized that the government did not want them to talk about the POW Issue, and that the government had no intention of following leads they had presented. Both of them, in a class action suit against President Ronald Reagan, charged him with failure to enforce the law of the land. When Smith was interviewed by Bill Bradley on *60 Minutes* he was asked why he would sue the President. He responded: "Don't get me wrong. I like Ronald Reagan. But he *is* the commander in chief. And this is a matter of honor."

The views of President Reagan's National Security Advisor Robert C. McFarlane differed from his boss. He said, in reference to the POW/MIA Issue, "The persistent wound  the lasting damage of Vietnam—is our ability to trust our government. And that won't go away until our government starts being honest with us again."

The class action suit was aimed at forcing the government to release information on all those men being held against their will. The suit declares that President Reagan, Defense Secretary Casper Weinberger, and Defense Intelligence Agency Director General James A. Williams and those who preceded these men in their jobs failed to enforce Title 22, United States Code. Section 1732 of Title 22 USC stipulates that *"whenever it is made known to the President that any citizen of the United States has been unjustly deprived of his liberty by or under the authority of any foreign government, it shall be the duty of the President forthwith to . . . use such means, not amounting to acts of war, as he may think necessary and proper to obtain "release."*

The question being asked was: did our government hide the fact that they had solid information on the POWs? Was our government in such a hurry to disengage from the longest, most divisive and frustrating foreign war in its history that it simply declared many of our POWs dead without launching a serious operation to rescue them? Did our government, once it learned of the existence and location of POWs try to discredit the would-be rescuers? To these questions Major Smith and Sergeant McIntyre replied, "Yes."

Joining Smith and McIntyre in the class action suit were Mrs. Dorothy Shelton, whose husband, Colonel Charles E. Shelton was a POW, Kathryn Fanning, wife of Capt. Hugh Fanning, who was suspicious that her husband's remains were not the ones she received from the government, and Anne Hart, wife of Lt. Col. Thomas T. Hart, who kept receiving a variety of reports about her husband. Her affidavit read: "Frequently one report would contradict another report. . . . I have been either intentionally or negligently misinformed." Jerry Dennis, brother of Navy corpsman Mark Dennis. Jerry had Mark's remains examined by civilian pathologists who concluded that they belonged to a 5'5" man. Mark was at least 5'11" tall.

Supporting the claims of those bringing the suit were: Dr. Michael Charney, a forensic anthropologist for 47 years, and Colonel Robert Lewis Howard, a Congressional Medal of Honor recipient and the Army's most decorated soldier. Both Smith and

McIntyre were convinced that the DIA, in order to escape its own liability in these cases, wanted to suppress and discredit people like themselves, people who had firsthand knowledge about the existence of POWs and wanted to act on it.

Kerry visited Vietnam and lavished praise on the regime, assuring the press who covered his visit that there's no believable evidence to back up the stories of live POWs still being held. Ironically, and worse, evidence of live POWs had been brought both to McCain and Kerry and every other member of the Committee in great abundance during the life of the Committee. While he and McCain worked strenuously to assist the Vietnamese, they were holding back, even destroying, as we have seen, vital information about our POWs. Kerry together with Senators John McCain, Nancy Kirshenbaum and Tom Daschle, appear to have worked very hard to block evidence from being made public. McCain argued during the embargo debate that the key to the democratization of Vietnam lay in giving them diplomatic recognition.

Coincidence?

Is it just coincidental that John Forbes Kerry's cousin, a Mr. Forbes, after the embargo was lifted, received exclusive rights to deal with any real estate transactions between North Vietnam and the United States government? According to the nonpartisan Center for Public Integrity, "Hanoi announced that it had awarded Colliers International, a Boston-based real estate, company, an exclusive deal to develop its commercial real estate potentially worth billions. Stuart Forbes, the CEO of Colliers, is [John] Kerry's cousin."

Was it a coincidence that the McCain family holds a large interest in the Budweiser Corporation and that Bud was among the first large U.S. corporations to enter Vietnam after relations were normalized? I have heard of too many politicians who give quid pro quos to be convinced that there was no connection between McCain's and Kerry's strong and vigorous pursuit of diplomatic normalization with Vietnam, in spite of the fact that POWs remained unaccounted for. To buttress, if it needs any buttressing, the argument that POW/MIA families were and are unable to get information about their loved ones, information that does exist in government files, read in the next chapter the Senate Select Committee testimony given by the startling Gaines Report. But first, another email from a POW family:

> From: MIA68VN@aol.com
> Date: Wed, 4 Apr 2007 19:00:04 EDT
> Subject: POW/MIAs
> To:  pajbascio@yahoo.com
> CC: sjclark@psyber.com

Dear Father Pat:

Summarizing 39 years of waiting and digging for the truth on the POW/MIA Issue is very difficult. It took Sue and I quite a bit of time to pare down our manuscript to a mere 1,000 pages which translated into a 476 page book. I will give you a few of my main thoughts without delving into the particulars of Jim's story as you can get those from the book.

Much of the frustration in trying to connect the dots with this Issue can be blamed upon the government's superb technique of compartmentalizing information. When you finally find someone who honestly wants to help find information for you, they run into roadblocks, too. Even men who were involved in some part of the story either have no idea what the outcome was or they will hypothesize the answer while standing on their laurels. Several times I've shown these people more pieces to the puzzle, pieces they've never seen or heard about. Their response is universal. They admit that they just presumed that the information they were responsible for reached the right person and was acted on appropriately. And, if you're dealing with information on someone who was in Special Forces and Special Operations then you are also up against the veil of secrecy.

My biggest disappointment came when I realized that there really wasn't an advocate in the government for my husband or any one of the POW/MIAs. As information slowly filters in about your particular case no one in your branch of service does anything more than just file that piece of paper. No one takes the time to analyze the information and possibly ask pertinent questions. It is up to the family members to do all of this. We have had to become the chief investigators and analytical experts for each of our cases. It is up to you to research, interview, document, and push for answers. And, you must be strong enough not to show your emotions and stand your ground when dealing with the government officials.

This journey has been an enlightening, amazing, sorrowful, frustrating, and demanding one. For years, I asked God why I was chosen to walk this path. I felt alone and betrayed just as Jesus did. Couldn't He just give me the answer to what happened to Jim? I've finally accepted that I've been chosen for a mission that I may never know the reason for. That maybe the people I meet as a result of this "issue" are the reason I'm walking this path.

If all this isn't bad enough, I came under government harassment for merely looking for the truth and telling the public what I'd found out. Please be sure and read Chapter 23 in my book as it details just how far they will go to try and stop me from talking. It's shocking to think that the very government my husband fought for was now turning on me because I wanted to know what happened to him.

I've attached a flyer that I use for advertising and you can go to www.is-anybody-listening.com, my website,  for more information.

Best of luck on your manuscript.

Sincerely,<br>Barbara Burchim

**ENDNOTE:**

1 Dr. Roger Shields of the office of the Assistant Secretary (ISA) Roger Shields. He headed up the overall Department of Defense coordination responsibility for all PW/MIA matters.

# CHAPTER FOUR

# TRADERS IN BODIES & DOG TAGS

**DEAN BERNAL IS FAR FROM BEING A PERSON** who delves into politics. His love is wildlife and the preservation of the environment. He primarily focuses his work since 1984 with JoJo, a wild dolphin, and marine conservation in the Turks and Caicos Islands, where he implemented his first whale research program for the Turks and Caicos Islands. He also is Founder and Executive Director, The Marine Wildlife Foundation, a U.S.-based non-profit organization with both U.S. and international programs. As if that is not enough, Dean is also Co-Founder and Co-Director of the Egypt Dolphin Conservation Project and the Documentary Video Production on Red Sea Dolphins. He is also Founder of the Norway Dolphin Project in programs for the legal protection, medical attention, public education and studies for the protection of Norway's lone dolphin.

Dean's connection with Vietnam was totally accidental. He spoke with Father Pat about the connection at the home of a mutual friend, Henry Mensen, in Henry's home on Ambergris Island, in the Caribbean. Dean's parents, he said, and nearly all of their closest friends, all senior citizens, had invested their life savings in a company owned by a Vietnamese businessman, Quand Dang Truong, now an American citizen. Truong was CEO and Chairman of IE One Company in San Jose, California. The company is in the heart of Silicon Valley, the dot com mecca of the world. Dean learned that his parents and their friends had been conned by Mr. Truong, so he decided to investigate what was going on. He did this by meeting with Quand in June of 2001and pretended that he was interested in investing in his company. He recalls: "Quand smiled and nodded at me a lot while reassuring me that an investment in his company was the best investment around but he didn't know I was doing an investigation on him and his company for fraud."

During his research on the company, he found that Quand had not disclosed that there was a suit filed with the Superior Court in California, County of Santa Clara, filed January 8th, 2001 against IE ONE. [Case number CV795044 which specifies the causes of Action as: 1) Breach of Contract, Damages; 2) Breach of Contract-specific performance; 3) Fraud.]

Dean discovered that Quand had committed fraud and stolen the savings and retirement monies of many senior citizens. Quand Dang and his partner, Nick Duong were pretty sly and had many impressive, or supposedly impressive, certificates on the office walls. Both Quand Dang and Nick Duong were of Vietnamese Nationality living and working with U.S. citizenship and residing in California.

Quand Dang Truong had international projects in China, Russia, the Philippines and Fiji, law and finance, not only in the U.S. but also in Russia and Taiwan. He received his education in law from Saigon University and Santa Clara University Law School. Nick Duong's specialty was project management, real state management, budget administration, import-export, and marketing for such companies as: Nafa Corporation, Vaco, Oxbow, Qualcomm, and IeOne Corp. He was educated in Vietnamese and U.S. universities.

Dean commented, "I had seen the likes of people like Quand and his entourage during my travels of the world. Living the greater part of my life in the Turks and Caicos Islands and witnessing many offshore schemes, I was aware of many schemes and how they proliferate among false hype and hope. Quand was no more to me than a sophisticated thief with a smile and law degree that allowed him to get away with it."

Hoping to help his parents and their friends, Dean approached the local police department but they needed more evidence before they would be willing to look into the matter. Not even the local TV news stations were interested in his story for the same reason. "Bring us the proof," was their response. "The investigative news stations told me that this type of crime happens so often in Silicon Valley that it's not a new news story to cover. I guess I would just go through the process of collecting information and get as much information out of Quand as I could while I was still able to speak to him. Speaking to Quand as a knowledgeable investor, my goal was to get Quand's trust and also his companies' bank account information and the opportunity to meet past investors, even prospective new investors." During this exercise, Dean befriended Quand personally, winning his trust. Gradually Dean got to know the network of the extensive still growing list of investors. The list kept getting bigger and bigger but little did anybody know of the consequences of their retirement funds being taken away from them. More important than getting to know his investors was to get to know his family, his kids, his wife and his closest family friends. Quand was a real work of art though and could easily convince people of his company's success or promise of success. It seemed every new group of investors was offered a new project investment from IE One. This new project investment fit the perfect needs of the investors and came with a guarantee from Quand personally that the company would triple their retirement monies in a matter of months.

At one meeting, Quand introduced Dean to his project manager, Nick Duang. Quand explained that Duang was a close business associate and personal friend, a man very well connected in Vietnam. "Quand asked me to sign a confidentiality agreement because we were going to be discussing sensitive information. I signed the agreement." Duang presented a folder to us that Quand was already familiar with. "I could tell Quand was familiar with the folder because he requested to see specific items before Duang opened the folder. He was requesting to see photos which were quickly handed over to him in a separate envelope." Quand asked Dean if he was interested in going to Vietnam with them and a couple investors in order to film the remains of MIA's from the Vietnam War. He showed him photos of two truck-size containers and in the containers were the remains of U.S. soldiers. Some photos were photos of the containers with the doors fully opened, displaying a large amount of U.S. military gear and human remains.

Dean recalls: "He also showed me close-up photos of the same military photos but closer to the human remains and U.S. military gear. There were about four photos of the containers from a distance seemingly recently unburied, dug up from the surrounding areas. Each container was a quarter of the way full at the doors of the container and about half-way full near the back of the container. The containers had illegible Asian lettering."

As Quand translated his Vietnamese partner's words, he presented and explained even more photos. "As the man spoke in Vietnamese and pointed to the pictures he waited for a response from me. But Quand had to finish translating." In the meantime, the man pointed to the details in the photos. One photo was a close-up of a U.S. dog tag on one of the remains. There were also many close-up photos of a pile of dog tags. He also showed Dean a photo of a human skull and as Quand translated, the Vietnamese man repeated, "U.S. Soldier, Vietnam" and continued to pound his finger on the photo and then rub his fingers together like money and then signed with his hands to give him money. Pointing to Dean, he said: "You can make lots of money," meaning of course, the re-sale of them to the POW families. Quand translated the Vietnamese man's words. "If you give me the money then I can get you the bodies and materials and proof that each body is a U.S. soldier's that is still today an MIA. We have all the dog tags, hair, glasses, and even personal letters and finger prints on cigarettes and letters and pictures from the pockets of the soldiers. We have everything from the U.S. soldiers. It's worth a lot of money to the U.S. government and you can buy the bodies and sell them to the U.S. government for lots of money,"

Quand explained in English to Dean that the Vietnamese people were aware that if a U.S. soldier was shot and killed, his body, IDs and clothing were worth a good deal of money to the U.S. government. The Vietnamese would sometimes take the body of an American that was killed in battle and bury the body in a discreet location. Later when other U.S. troops would come near the village areas the Vietnamese could use the hidden remains to bargain with the U.S. soldiers for money or, if need be, their own lives. It was a touchy situation because there was always the accusation of who killed the American soldier and why?

The Vietnamese mafia was determined that if money was going to be made on the bodies of American soldiers then it would be money for them. They took advantage of the fact that there were so many American bodies, hundreds of them, that an organized group alone would be able to provide the containers to absorb them all. Also needed were the governmental and international connections to see that they were organized into a consistently flourishing money-making business, marked by a larger organized method of systemized collection. This collection was completed by the Vietnamese mafia themselves as they entered villages and threatened the lives of villagers who they thought may have buried American soldiers' bodies. The villagers would bury the bodies for hiding and safe keeping in hopes of receiving money for identifying the locations of their claim or claims. But when the mafia arrived they would use effective methods of interrogations, tortures and even take the life of a villager in order to discover the locations of the American soldiers' remains.

Quand explained to Dean that some of the villages were even pre-organized to take the bodies of American soldiers for the mafia in the case any U.S. soldiers were killed in the area. It was explained to me that this is why the soldiers and much of their gear were still intact. It was mandated by the Vietnamese mafia that all the belongings of the soldier had to be intact. This explained the unusual completeness of many of the soldiers' personal belongings such as letters, pictures, their dog tags and other military gear. The bodies would then be dug up from their temporary graves where they were buried and brought to the containers for a later sale. The idea was to sell them to Americans and then rebury them in mass containers to later be exhumed again for sale to the highest bidders on the black market. Quand assured me that I could become very rich because, since he liked me personally and, since he worked closely with the Vietnamese mafia, he would see to it that I got preferential treatment. "Quand then asked me if I would like to come to Vietnam and film the containers and document all the bodies so we could sell it to the U.S. government after he bought the U.S. human remains. He wanted the whole process documented from the time we arrived to the time we departed Vietnam. He also told me he knew many officials in Vietnam so we wouldn't have to worry if something went wrong. I continued to show an interest in the filming of the containers and the U.S. soldiers' human contents. Quand spoke about how famous we would be for recovering the MIA soldiers and bringing them home." And, as for the profit to be made, he estimated that because the U.S. government would purchase the bodies from him personally, he would see to it that the U.S. pays for the shipping of all the bodies home. This would bring him and Dean a 1,000 percent markup on the purchase. The base price for each American remains would be in the high hundreds of thousands, especially since the POW families would be pressuring in the government to pay any price for the return of these American heroes. The profits therefore would be almost beyond imagination.

He then read to Dean one of the photographed letters from one of the dead soldiers' pockets written to the soldier's wife. With the letter, there was a photograph of his dog tag and other military ID, and a photo of a child from his pocket.

> "He showed me many photos of dog tags that he said he already looked up in government documents and could see they were the dog tags of MIA that have not been recovered. He suggested I should take the name and numbers and look them up myself so I could see they are still MIA." Quand then said that he had one partner in the U.S. military, a general, who confirmed the authenticity of the MIA dog tags and the authenticity of the photos and names and dates of the letters. Even though he was in the military, Quand explained, he was not working as military personnel but acting as a primary investor who would also get profit out of the deal. Quand asked Dean what month would be the most convenient month he could leave for Vietnam and stay to

film for three weeks. He quickly remarked that
the tapes would have to be shipped back separately just for safe keeping. Once all was documented, he said, he and Dean could get investors
together for the initial purchase of the bodies to
guarantee his ownership. After that had taken
place, then Quand would sell them to the U.S.
government, take his share and then give the bal-
ance of the money to the investor or investors,
i.e., either Dean alone, if he were the lone investor, or Dean and others if there were others.

"I then surprised Quand by insisting that before I put out my money, I needed to see the annual reports on his company, so that I could
verify his financial statements. Within two weeks
the office was empty and Quand disappeared."

And so it was and so it is that the long forgotten heroes of over 30 years ago and their families,
together with those who died in battle more recently, cannot find closure either because of po
litical or economic gain on the part of a few. It is
a sad state of affairs and I weep for it.

—Dean Bernal

## LEGAL FILES

Quang Dang Truong, CEO/Chairman. Nick Duong and Jack
Le

It is case number 01 208 9714, San Jose Police Dept., date of
file 7-27-01 . . . Badge number 3389.

Dean Bernal filed this case in San Jose, Ca. because Quand
Truong lied about the company, investors and finances to Dean
Bernal and did not disclose prior law suits against the company.

Also be aware that there was a suit filed with the Superior
Court in California, County of Santa Clara, filed January 8th,
2001 against IE ONE, case number CV795044, which specifies
the causes of Action as: 1) Breach of Contract, Damages;

2) Breach of Contract-specific performance; 3) Fraud, Promise without intent to perform.

The following resignation letter of Colonel Millard Peck will break your heart to read, but it can also strengthen your resolve to join the chorus of POW/MIA families for answers to their painful wait for news and/or closure to the lives of their loved ones:

### Colonel Peck's Memorandum of Resignation

DATE: 12 FEB 1991
ATTN: POW-MIA
SUBJECT: Request for Relief
TO: DR

1. PURPOSE: I, hereby, request to resign my position as Chief of the Special Office for Prisoners of War and Missing in Action (POW-MIA).

2. BACKGROUND:

a. Motivation. My initial acceptance of this posting was based upon two primary motives; first, I had heard that the job was highly contentious and extremely frustrating, that no one would volunteer for it because of its complex political nature. This, of course, made it appear challenging. Secondly, since the end of the Vietnam War, I had heard the persistent rumors of American servicemen having been abandoned in Indochina, and that the Government was conducting a "cover-up" so as not to be embarrassed. I was curious about this and thought that serving as the Chief of POW-MIA would be an opportunity to satisfy my own interest and help clear the Government's name.

b. The Office's Reputation. It was interesting

that my previous exposure to the POW- MIA Office, while assigned to DIA, both as a Duty Director for Intelligence (DDI) and as the Chief of the Asia Division for Current Intelligence (JSI -3), was negative. DIA personnel, who worked for me, when dealing with or mentioning the Office, always spoke about it in deprecating tones, alluding to the fact that any report which found its way there would quickly disappear into a "black hole."

c. General Attitudes. Additionally, surveys of active duty military personnel indicated that a high percentage (83%) believed that there were still live American prisoners in Vietnam. This idea was further promulgated in a number of legitimate veterans' periodicals and professional journals, as well as the media in general, which held that where there was so much smoke, there must be fire.

d. Cover-up. The dark side of the Issue was particularly unsettling because of the persistent rumors and innuendoes of a Government conspiracy, alleging that U.S. military personnel had been left behind to the victorious communist governments in Vietnam, Laos and Cambodia, and that for "political reasons" or running the risk of a second Vietnam War, their existence was officially denied. Worse yet was the implication that DIA's Special Office for POWs and MIAs was an integral part of this effort to cover the entire affair up so as not to embarrass the Government nor the Defense Establishment.

e. The Crusade. As a Vietnam veteran with a certain amount of experience in Indochina, I was interested in the entire POW-MIA question, and willingly volunteered for the job, viewing it as sort of a holy crusade.

f. The Harsh Reality. Heading up the Office

has not been pleasant. My plan was to be totally honest and forthcoming on the entire issue and aggressively pursue innovative actions and concepts to clear up the live sighting business, thereby refurbishing the image and honor of DIA. I became painfully aware, however, that I was not really in charge of my own office, but was merely a figurehead or whipping boy for a larger and totally Machiavellian group of players outside of DIA. What I witnessed during my tenure as the cardboard cut-out "Chief" of POW-MIA could be euphemistically labeled as disillusioning.

3. CURRENT IMPRESSIONS, BASED ON MY EXPERIENCE:

a. Highest National Priority. That National leaders hypocritically continue to address the prisoner of war and missing in action issue as the "highest national priority" is a travesty. From my vantage point, I observed that the principal government players were interested primarily in conducting a "damage limitation exercise," and appeared to knowingly and deliberately generate an endless succession of manufactured crises and "busy work." Progress consisted in frenetic activity, with little substance and no real results.

b. The Mindset to Debunk. The mindset to "debunk" is alive and well. It is held at all levels, and continues to pervade the POW-MIA Office, which is not necessarily the fault of DIA. Practically all analysis is directed to finding fault with the source. Rarely has there been any effective, active follow through on any of the sightings, nor is there a responsive "action arm" to routinely and aggressively pursue leads. The latter was a moot point, anyway, since the Office was continuously buried in an avalanche of "ad hoc" taskings from every quarter, all of which required an immediate response. It was impossible to plan ahead or prioritize courses of action. Any real effort to pursue live sighting reports or exercise initiatives was diminished by the plethora of "busy work" projects directed by higher authority outside of DIA. A number of these grandiose endeavors bordered on the ridiculous, and—quite significantly—there was never an audit trail. None of these taskings was ever requested formally. There was, and still is, a refusal by any of the players to follow normal intelligence channels in dealing with the POW-MIA Office.

c. Duty, Honor and Integrity. It appears that the entire issue is being manipulated by unscrupulous people in the Government, or associated with the Government. Some are using the issue for personal or political advantage and others use it as a forum to perform and feel important, or worse. The sad fact, however, is that this issue is being controlled and a cover-up may be in progress. The entire charade does not appear to be an honest effort, and may never have been.

d. POW-MIA Officers Abandoned. When I assumed the Office for the first time, I was somewhat amazed and greatly disturbed by the fact that I was the only military officer in an organization of more than 40 people. Since combatants of all Services were lost in Vietnam, I would have thought there would at least be a token Service representation for a matter of the "highest national priority." Since the normal mix of officers from all Services is not found in my organization it would appear that the issue, at least at the working level, has, in fact, been abandoned. Also, horror stories of the succession of military officers at the 0-5 and 0-6 level who have in some manner "rocked the boat" and quickly come to grief at the hands of the Government policy makers who direct the issue, lead one to the conclusion that we are all quite expendable, so by extrapolation one simply concludes that these same bureaucrats would "sacrifice" anyone who was troublesome or contentious as including prisoners of war and missing in action. Not a comforting thought. Any military officer expected to survive in this environment would have to be myopic, an accomplished sycophant, or totally insouciant.

e. The DIA Involvement. DIA's role in the affair is truly unfortunate. The overall Agency has generally practiced a "damage limitation drill" on the issue, as well. The POW-MIA Office has been cloistered for all practical purposes and left to its own fortunes. The POW Office is the lowest level in the Government "efforts" to resolve the issue, and oddly for an intelligence organization, has become the "lightning rod" for the entire establishment to the matter. The policy people manipulating the affair have maintained their distance and remained hidden in the shadows, while using the Office as a "toxic waste dump" to bury the whole "mess" out of sight and mind to a facility with limited access to public scrutiny. Whatever happens in the issue, DIA takes the blame, while the real players remain invisible. The fact that the POW-MIA Office is always the center of an investigation is no surprise. Many people suspect that something is rotten about the whole thing, but they cannot find an audit trail to ascribe blame, so they attack the DIA/POW-MIA "dump," simply because it has been placed in the line of fire as a cheap, expendable decoy.

f. "*Suppressio Veri, Suggestio Falsi.*" Many of the puppet masters play a confusing, murky role. For instance, the Director of the National League of Families occupies an interesting and questionable position in the whole process. Although assiduously "churning" the account to give a tawdry illusion of progress, she is adamantly opposed to any initiative to actually get to the heart of the problem, and, more importantly, interferes in or actively sabotages POW-MIA analyses or investigations. She insists on rewriting or editing all significant documents produced by the Office, then touted as the DIA position. She apparently has access to top secret, codeword message traffic, for which she is supposedly not cleared, and she receives it well ahead of the DIA intelligence analysts. Her influence in "jerking around" everyone and everything involved in the issue goes far beyond the "war and MIA protester gone straight" scenario. She was brought from the "outside," into the center of the imbroglio, and then, cloaked in a mantle of sanctimony, routinely impedes real progress and insidiously "muddles up" the issue. One wonders who she really is and where she came from.

4. CONCLUSIONS:

a. The Stalled Crusade. Unfortunately, what began on such a high note never succeeded in embarking. In some respects, however, I have managed to satisfy some of my curiosity.

b. Everyone is Expendable. I have seen first-hand how ready and willing the policy people are to sacrifice or "abandon" anyone who might be perceived as a political liability. It is quick and facile, and can be easily covered.

c. High-Level Knavery. I feel strongly that this issue is being manipulated and controlled at a higher level, not with the goal of resolving it, but more to obfuscate the question of live prisoners, and give the illusion of progress through hyperactivity.

d. "Smoke and Mirrors." From what I have witnessed, it appears that any soldier left in Vietnam, even inadvertently was, in fact, abandoned years ago, and that the farce that is being played is no more than political legerdemain done with "smoke and mirrors," to stall the issue until it dies a natural death.

e. National League of Families. I am convinced that the Director of this organization is much more than meets the eye. As the principal actor in the grand show, she is in the perfect position to clamor for "progress," while really intentionally impeding the effort. And there are numerous examples of this. Otherwise it is inconceivable that so many bureaucrats in the "system" would instantaneously do her bidding and humor her every whim.

f. DIA's Dilemma. Although greatly saddened by the role ascribed to the Defense Intelligence Agency, I feel, at least, that I am dealing with honest men and women who are generally powerless to make the system work. My appeal and attempt to amend this role perhaps never had a chance. We all were subject to control. I particularly salute the personnel in the POW-MIA Office for their long suffering, which I regrettably was unable to change. I feel that the Agency and the Office are being used as the "fall guys" or "patsies" to cover the tracks of others.

## 5. RECOMMENDATIONS:

a. One Final Vietnam Casualty. So ends the war and my last grand crusade, like it actually did end, I guess. However, as they say in the Legion, *"je ne regrette rien . . . "* For all of the above, I respectfully request to be relieved of my duties as Chief of the Special Office for Prisoners of War and Missing in Action.

b. A Farewell to Arms. So as to avoid the annoyance of being shipped off to some remote corner, out of sight and out of the way, in my own "bamboo cage" of silence somewhere, I further request that the Defense Intelligence Agency, which I have attempted to serve loyally and with honor, assist me in being retired immediately from active military duty.

—MILLARD A. PECK
Colonel, Infantry
USA

HOME
BY
1964 1968 1972 1976

# CHAPTER FIVE

# BOBBY GARWOOD

*This chapter was written exclusively by John Holland. He has been a friend of Bobby Garwood for years.*

**I HAVE KNOWN BOBBY GARWOOD** for more than twenty years, and I consider him a very good friend. People find that rather unusual, as I am a retired Sergeant Major and he is a dishonorably discharged Marine. I do not find it odd nor unusual, as I have many friends and close associates that are very different from the "run of the mill" populace. I try to judge people by what I see on all sides of them, and I try not to be "taken in" by the side they want to show me. I have many reasons to personally believe that Bob is a very good American and should be held as an icon to anyone who serves in the U.S. military, and especially any who may become a prisoner of war. I also believe that Bob is, undoubtedly, the most maligned person in the United States today. I do not have a great amount of knowledge about the particulars of military justice; however I have enough knowledge to recognize injustice when I see it. It is my belief that Bob has been wrongly accused and convicted, on trumped-up charges, in order to cover the combined tails of many "personages of high status" who are deeply involved in the POW/MIA cover-up.

When Bobby Garwood returned to the U.S. in 1979, after nearly fourteen years as a POW, he became an embarrassment to the U.S. Government. After all, the government had, at that time, recently announced that "there are no American Service Personnel left in Vietnam." The fallaciousness of this statement was that only a year before, the government had received a message from Bob (the first that Bob had been able to smuggle out).

Members of the National Security Council had discussed this message on several occasions and a member of the Council (Col. Robert McFarlane) later told of the discussions. (And still, the government said no one was there! That is absolute perfidy!)

To add fuel to that fire, between the time that the government got the first message, and the time Bob got out, the government had sent two Marine officers to Greensburg, Indiana, to try to get Bob's dad (Jack) to sign papers admitting that he believed Bob to be dead. As a carrot to lead Bob's dad, they offered him $90,000 as Bob's back pay and allowances (the importance of this offer will be shown later!). Bob's dad, who had not received any word, directly from Bob, for more than thirteen years, refused the payment and refused to sign because he believed that Bob was still alive, and he also suspected that the government knew something they were not telling him. (Jack and I discussed this subject on two separate occasions.)

Bob Garwood went to Vietnam in 1965, when the 3rd Marine Division was deployed there from Okinawa, Japan. At the time he was captured he was a nineteen-year-old private with a couple of years in the Corps, a small town country boy who had joined very young and was looking forward to getting out, getting home, and getting married. In fact the date of the marriage had already been set. On September 28, 1965, twelve days before he was due to rotate home for discharge, he became a Prisoner of War. He was assigned as a driver in the division motor pool, when he was captured in the vicinity of Da Nang, South Vietnam, by an element of the Viet Cong. He had been detailed to pick up an officer at an outpost and deliver him to the airport, when he became lost and strayed into a Viet Cong controlled village. Bob resisted capture with the .45 cal pistol with which he was armed. It is believed that Bob killed at least one VC, before he became wounded and captured. The facts that he was carrying a pistol and the vehicle had divisional markings on the bumpers, led the VC to believe they had captured an officer. Initially this mistake saved his life, but later this caused Bob grief when he denied he was an officer.

At first the Marine Corps thought that Bob could have gone

AWOL, however that was soon proven wrong, and early on it was declared that he had become a POW. His vehicle was found along with spent shell casings from his .45. Also there were people in the village who saw him captured. Years later, long after Bob was court-martialed, a picture surfaced that had been taken shortly after his capture. It showed Bob in his white under shorts with a freshly wrapped bandage on his forearm, and his hands tied together. Bob had no idea that this picture had been taken and was very surprised to see it. I happened to be with Bob, at the place where he was then employed, when Mike Van Atta showed him the picture. The picture should have been given to his defense attorney, but had not been. Why? Well, this was just one of the things that should have been given to the defense attorney, but wasn't. I have no idea where Mike got the picture, and if he told Bob I never learned. The picture should have been in Bob's files, but then again, his defense attorney had never had access to his files!

For a year or so Bob was held captive in bamboo cages in a jungle POW camp. He was the only American until Captain Eisenbraun, U.S. Army, arrived. Captain Eisenbraun had spent several tours in Vietnam with Special Forces, and had returned as an advisor with MACV. He had been captured on July 5 1965, before Bob, but had been held elsewhere for awhile. He was very fluent in Vietnamese and insisted that Bob learn the language, which Bob did, surprisingly fast. (Remember this—he was ordered to learn the language!). The next prisoner to arrive was Corporal Russell Grissett, a recon Marine, whose main thoughts had been to get home to his mother and sister. Corporal Grissett had been captured Jan 22 1966. These three were together for more than a year before Captain Eisenbraun did something, or refused to do something, that made the Vietnamese mad at him. Then, they beat him to death, breaking several bones in his body in the process. Bob and Russ buried the captain and marked his grave. They later had to bury several other POWs in the same area. The other bodies have all been returned, thanks to Bob's description of where they were located. For some reason, the Vietnamese have never returned Captain Eisenbraun's body. The

Vietnamese reported that he died in captivity from a "fall."

During 1966-1969, after American ground troops were brought into the war, many American POWs were brought to the camp where Bob and Russ were held. Bob, because of his language ability, had been, more or less, drafted as an interpreter for the camp and as a result some of the prisoners thought he had "turned." Anyone with experience with interpreters recognizes that when there is a good one around, it is normal for the group for which the interpreter works to accept him as "one of us." (Even our "vaunted news media" was taken in this way. A Vietnamese "journalist" with good language capabilities was epitomized to the degree that he attended South Vietnamese government briefings with the U.S. journalists, and many stories were taken to him for clarification. His versions were accepted over the versions of the South Vietnamese Government. After the war, this man became a member of the Communist Vietnamese government. All along, he had been a spy!  Inexperienced soldiers, as most of these POWs were, never knew or realized that this phenomenon existed, nor that it was happening right before their eyes, so several thought Bob was actively collaborating. Actually, Bob was using his position to help the other POWs as much as he could, as he was able to get things for the others that they could not get for themselves, and this included some food and medicines, as well as information he gained by listening when the guards played their personal radios. During this period there was an incident that shows how some POWs are so self-centered that they think only of themselves even to the detriment of the others. Others do just the opposite; they sacrifice themselves for the good of the others. An example of this happened when Bob's friend Russ became sick with malaria. Bob took his own life in his hands when he stole quinine and other medicines for Russ. Because of his status as "interpreter" he was not allowed free access to the general compound with the other prisoners, so he entrusted the medicines to the only U.S. Army medical doctor that the Viet Cong held during the Vietnam War, asking him to give it to Russ. It was only after Russ died that Bob learned that the doctor had not given the medicine to Russ, but had taken it himself as "preventative medicine." This had left Russ in a more weakened condition than if he had the quinine. Guards had taken Bob and a couple of other POWs out of the camp for a couple of days on food gathering detail. When he returned from this detail he learned that Russ had been badly beaten after he admitted to killing and eating the camp commander's cat. (Actually several other POWs had participated in the killing and the feast, but Russ did not give-up their names). When Bob learned that Russ was in "bad shape," he started running into the hut, and inadvertently pushed another POW with his forearm, causing him to step back and off of a step. Russ died shortly after Bob got to him. Bob was later charged with physically attacking this POW, an offense that merits several years of jail time. The POW himself went against instructions at the court-martial, and defended Bob's action, and the charge was reduced to "simple assault" (an offense that is usually handled by an Article 15, administrative punishment, or a minor type of court-martial).

In 1969, the North Vietnamese started moving the POWs held by the Viet Cong in South Vietnam to North Vietnam. Bob was separated from the other Americans during this move and was moved with South Vietnamese POWs. He was separated from them one night, and told to expect to be executed. Why was he to be executed? He never learned. While he was separated the camp was bombed, killing all of the South Vietnamese POWs and the guards. Bob, who had been alone in a hut, was seriously injured. Unconscious, he lost a good bit of time, how much he doesn't know. He came to himself in a North Vietnamese hospital, and they thought he was a Cuban, as at that time Castro and a large group of his minions were running around North Vietnam. (During his visit to North Vietnam, Castro actually went across the 17th parallel into South Vietnam, and attended a meeting at a North Vietnamese military base!)

At several points Bob was accused of carrying weapons for the Vietnamese, and there is actually a film of him and a couple of others holding weapons, but they were handed to them as it was being filmed and it was easy to see that it was an unusual happening.  The POWs were startled when they were handed the weapons. On another occasion Bob was on a work detail when one of the guards became sick, and his weapon was dismantled and placed in Bob's back pack. These incidents were used at Bob's court-martial to prove collaboration.

After Bob reached North Vietnam, he was mostly held separately from other POWs, although occasionally he would see them and was able to talk to several. He heard on Vietnamese radio, through a loudspeaker, that President Nixon had said that all of the American POWs were home. That was when he first knew (and it came as a terrible shock to him) that he had been abandoned. Bob, like most Americans, had never heard of the large scale abandonment of American POWs (who had been held in German POW Camps). These Americans were "liberated" by the Soviets at the end World War II, and then taken to the Soviet Union's notorious prison gulag. These 20,000 to 30,000 Americans were never released! Nor was Bob aware that thousands more American POWs had been abandoned to the Soviets, Chinese, and North Koreans after the Korean War, and have never been released.

After he was abandoned, Bob spent most of the remaining years of his captivity working in a motor pool, and doing other jobs as they were assigned to him. He traveled around, under guard, repairing vehicles and generators, and in his travels he saw many American POWs being held in different places. At one time he saw and heard American POWs getting off of a train and at another time he was taken, by boat, to what he thought was an island in a large man-made lake, to repair a generator. While he was there he saw several buildings where Caucasians were being held. He did not get to identify them as Americans, but they appeared to be living under guard. Later, when he returned to this location, with ex-Congressman Hendon and Senator Bob Smith, he went directly, through tall elephant grass, to the foundation of a building that matched the size and location of the one he described as housing the generators. The buildings that housed the Caucasians were exactly where he said they would be and they were constructed as he had said they were. Later the government tried to call him a liar because it was not a "true" island because "during low water times" there is a trail that leads from the land mass to the mainland. I guess the government thought Bob was on surveying trip, or a vacation, and had the liberty to explore the island to learn little facts like this. These same government people also must have never learned that jungle and forest can be cleared and crops like tea can be planted in the same place.

During this period Bob was also detailed to work for a person who, after he defected to the United States, became known as "The Mortician." This man was responsible for cleaning the bones of American remains, and storing them in a warehouse in Hanoi. There were more than 400 sets of remains in this warehouse, and thus far most of them have not been returned. During the time Bob worked for him, there were two other Americans who were also detailed to the job. After the Mortician reached the U.S., after defecting, he initially denied knowing Bob, even though he had told of the three Americans. Later, in a private conversation he admitted to Bob that he had realized what the U.S. Government was doing to Bob, and he was afraid that if he admitted knowing Bob, and saying something the government didn't want him to say, that he would be sent back to Vietnam. (In actuality, the U.S. Government treated the Mortician much the same as they did General Senja, who defected from Czechoslovakia. His every statement was found to be true, and was believed, except when he spoke of American POWs. In both instances, the U.S. Government refused the information about American POWs, and did not pursue the subject. In other words, THE COVER-UP TAKES PRECEDENCE OVER FIRST-HAND KNOWLEDGE!

While working temporarily on another job, Bob met a Chinese girl who was from Hanoi. She told him about a hotel in Hanoi where Westerners stayed, and about the items they could buy at a store in the hotel. Bob usually had the same driver and guard when he was detailed to travel around and repair motors, and he had became well acquainted with them. His trips had taken him by this hotel several times. Adding these factors together, Bob began to form a plan to escape. Knowing that he would be risking his life by even trying to escape, Bob was willing to risk every thing to get word back to our government that he was still alive and being held prisoner. Being a patriotic American, a member of the Armed Services (and thus trained to believe that "we leave no one behind"), he believed that our government would try its best to rescue him. He tried to figure out how to get a message to the States. This was at a time when even most hard core POW/MIA activists still had faith in our government and had not yet realized that when it came to abandoning POWs, our government was actually the "biggest duck-in-the-puddle." How could an abandoned American POW possibly know, or even imagine, that our government had people in charge that cared not about the abandoned POWs, or even the country as a whole, but were people with a self-centered private agenda. Bob made a deal with the guard and driver to get him some Westerner clothes, and to allow him to visit the hotel store alone. The items he brought out were sold on the black market. Bob accepted no money for his actions as he was not allowed to have money and did not wish to be caught with any. He was very cautious not to take any contraband back into his prison area for the same reason. Bob made several trips into the store before he heard a person speaking English and approached him. The man was a New Zealand journalist, who accepted Bob's message. Some say the journalist became scared and destroyed the message, but delivered it verbally, while others say the written message is still in the hands of the American government—I don't know. I do know that the message was discussed by members of the National Security Council, and then ignored. The second person, to whom Bob gave the message, was a Finnish officer in the World Bank. This man delivered the message to the U.S. government, but only after informing the British Broadcasting Company, and thus, the information was announced all over the world. The American government realized that it could not "get this cat back into the bag." Bob had to be brought home. Bob's traveling guard and the driver were executed almost immediately, ostensibly for black marketing. The night before Bob was allowed to leave North Vietnam he was taken to the outskirts of Hanoi, and forced to witness the execution of the Chinese girl, whose only crime was telling Bob about the hotel. Even when being released from illegal detention FREEDOM IS NEVER FREE! Bob could not believe that such punishment could be, or would be, meted out for what we Americans would consider to be only minor infractions. These executions will always wear hard on Bob's conscience.

Bob did make it back to the United States, and he expected to soon be a civilian and get on with the life that had been so long disrupted, but that was not to be. The people he had embarrassed had to have their "pound of flesh." He had to be punished for being alive when they said he was dead. He had to be punished for pulling back the curtain and showing that the "powers that be" were naked of honor and respect and cared not for the "common man nor the service man." Bob should have been hailed as the hero he was, but instead he was lambasted in the press and by our government. Bob, an under-educated country boy who had not even finished high school, had done what thousands of other abandoned POWs, many highly educated, were unable to do. All alone, he had pulled the wool over the eyes of the Vietnamese government, and had notified our government that he was actually alive (not once but twice). He had forced our government to bring him home, even though the leaders of our government did not want him, and had already abandoned him on more than one occasion. He was abandoned once, when our government made no effort to get a proper accounting of all POWs at the war's end. Then the government re-sentenced him to a lingering death by rejecting him after he had risked his very life to get out the first message. After Bob was finally returned home, he was dealt the worst ignominy of all, the government of the country he loved, let it be known that he was believed to be a deserter, who had willingly stayed in Vietnam. He was called a collaborator who had "gone over" to the communists, and other vile stories were circulated about him. He was investigated for desertion, even though there were witness statements that he had been seen being captured, and it was known that he had put up resistance. He was investigated for stealing the vehicle, even though the dispatch slip was in evidence. He was investigated for arranging the trip so he could desert. But another driver testified that he and Bob had raced to the vehicle dispatcher's window when it was announced that an "off post" trip was available, and Bob got there first. A couple of other ex-POWs also showed up at Bob's court-martial who wished to testify in his defense, but were refused. They were told that they would "be next" if they did. The actual excuse was, "they had not been deposed during the investigation," but then very few defense witnesses had been deposed, even the ones that Bob requested. Several of the prosecution witnesses were ex-POWs who had returned "under a cloud," and had been excused only by President Nixon's statement that no returned POW would be prosecuted. None of these ex-POWs had made any charges against Bob when they were initially debriefed, but had indicated that Bob had been treated the same as they had. Why Bob did not fall under President Nixon's "blanket of protection" has never been explained.

At Bob's court-martial he was found guilty of collaboration with the enemy in that he learned the language. (I know of a Marine Sergeant who was held by the Japanese during WWII and learned the Japanese language, so he could act as an interpreter, and he was awarded the Bronze Star for doing so.) Any person who doesn't learn a language, after more than thirteen years of daily exposure to it would have to have no language ability at all. And the main kicker to this charge was that he was ordered by a superior officer, Captain Eisenbraun, to learn the language! The fact that he had held a weapon and carried one (placed in his pack by a guard) was used to reinforce the charge of collaboration. Bob was also found guilty of simple assault because he pushed another POW off of the step, and this POW had testified that he had done it inadvertently. When he was found guilty, Bob was sentenced to be dishonorably discharged and to forfeit all pay due and to become due. This was one hell of a sentence, as Bob had not been paid since he was a driver in the 3rd Marine Division Motor Pool in 1965. Evan if Bob had deliberately committed the crimes for which he was found guilty, the sentence he received was completely outrageous! Anyone who thinks that the sentence matched the offense would agree that a hungry nine-year-old child should be hanged for stealing a loaf of bread.

Bob was held on duty for another year or two without pay! (Isn't that slavery?) Bob was eventually allowed to return to civilian life, but only as an unpaid Marine, waiting for his court-martial to be approved. I personally have never seen anything like it. I have never seen it take more than a couple of months for a court-martial to be approved. Remember that $90,000 that his dad had been offered? Bob never saw it! Jack told me that had he even dreamed that Bob could be treated in this manner he would have taken the money and banked it for him.

Even after Bob was dishonorably discharged, the government did not leave him alone, and it still doesn't. He has been followed and harassed by elements of our government that would still like to "get him" on something, or anything, to further discredit him in some manner. As ridiculous and unbelievable as this will sound, the U.S. government even tried to set him up by having a woman move in with him. The woman became acquainted with Bob through a person who admitted, while testifying at the Senate Select Committee hearing, that he had been hired as an agent provocateur to disrupt the POW/MIA activists in and around Washington, D.C. It is also believed that this person participated in the planning of this ruse by inviting Bob to come to North Carolina to live. Bob thought there was genuine affection in the relationship with the woman and had thoughts of possibly continuing the relationship indefinitely. The woman was passing herself off to Bob as a member of the North Carolina National Guard and had shown Bob her National Guard identification. Bob was working at a local car dealership, and one morning he had to return to the apartment, when he forgot his keys. As he came in the kitchen he heard her on the phone and heard her refer to the other person in the conversation by a name he recognized. At that time, he realized that she was talking to someone in the Department of Defense, and that she was talking about him. Naturally, he became incensed but, as is his usual demeanor, did nothing rash. Her purse was where she usually left it when she was in the house, and he went through it, looking for anything that might clarify the situation for him. He found a U.S. Army identification card that identified her as a first lieutenant in the

U.S. Army. Later, when he confronted her, she admitted that she had been detailed to "keep an eye on him." The agent provocateur's first name is Ted and the woman's first name is Karen.

Bob had been back nearly eight years when the Department of Defense decided to debrief him in detail. Bob was glad to finally get it done, and went freely. The debriefing lasted about two weeks. During the debriefing, Bob saw a newspaper that had a picture of an Arab diplomat that had recently been posted to the United Nations. Bob made a statement that he knew him and gave a different name for him than was used in the newspaper. The de-briefer told him that he had used the right name, but he wanted to know how Bob knew it. Bob told him that the diplomat was one of the Arabs that had come to Vietnam to learn how to interrogate Americans, and had used him, and other POWs, as training aids. That was also where Bob learned the rudiments of the Arabic language, and surprised Monica Jensen when he ordered, in Arabic, one night in an Afghan restaurant in Washington, DC.

The following paragraph is my opinion of what happened in Congress and I believe it all pertains to Bobby Garwood. I believe that Bob Garwood's return was the catalyst of all the Congressional actions that followed his "homecoming."

Senator Jesse Helms (R-NC) had his minority staff of the Senate Foreign Relations Committee investigate the POW/MIA Issue, and published a very definitive report on the subject. He had stated that he would investigate the matter very thoroughly. Then his term expired and he had a very tough fight and needed some help to hold his seat. Admiral Nance (USN Ret.), who had been working in the POW/MIA cover-up since he was a young officer, and who at this time was assigned to the National Security Council, left that post and went to Senator Helms' assistance. Funds that had been denied the Senator suddenly became available. Senator Helms was re-elected by a very slim margin and Admiral Nance became his chief of staff, replacing a man who had worked for the Senator for more than twenty-six years. The Senator fired him out of hand and apparently without a qualm. Admiral Nance's first job, as chief of staff, was to fire the entire minority staff of the Foreign Relations Committee. Senator Helms instantly lost all interest in the POW/MIA Issue, and nothing has ever been done with his excellent report, although Senator Smith did refer to it several times.

Senator Bob Smith (R-NH) was undoubtedly the greatest POW/MIA advocate in either house of Congress and he delved into the issue like no other politician ever has, and he was very effective in his efforts. He laid his life and career on the line every day of his time in the Senate. The Senator's efforts were not aimed at the recovery of the bodies of the dead MIAs and POWs. He firmly believed then, and still believes now, that there were thousands of live abandoned U.S. POWs after WWII, Korea, and Vietnam. The Senator's actions were instrumental in renewing interest in the POWs left in North Korea, China and the Soviet Union, who had been abandoned after the Korean War, and also those abandoned to the Soviet Union, after WWII. The Senator truly became an icon in the eyes of the POW/MIA activists when, on one of his trips to South Korea he, unofficially, crossed the border into North Korea to "ask a few questions." By entering North Korea, Senator Smith not only endangered his own life for the issue, but he went against U.S. government policies banning travel to that country. His great interest in the issue and his actions gave the issue of "Living Abandoned POWs" Senatorial acknowledgement, which it had not had until that time. The Senator was "rattling cages," sending negative messages about those who caused the POWs to be abandoned. This caused great fear in their ranks. That is what put Senator Smith on the "hit list" for the Republican Party. After twelve years as a Senator, two full terms, these heroic actions caused the party to support a "docile card-carrying family member" to defeat him in a primary election. It smacks of crooked politics. Thus, the Senator joined the ranks of Republican politicians who had been disenfranchised by the Republican Party because of their interest in the POW/MIA Issue. The Senator's disenfranchisement was preceded by those of Congressmen Billy Hendon of North Carolina and John Le Boutillier of New York, and was followed by Congressman Bob Dornan of California.

When Bob Garwood first returned, Congressmen Gillman of New York and Wolfe of Virginia were instrumental in bringing his story to the public. They were the first members of Congress to show interest in Bob's return. Later they remained "interested but not overly active" in the issue. In my opinion a lot of pressure was brought to bear on them! Because of their interest in the issue the first three Congressmen mentioned were actively scorned by the Republican Part and, they all, like Senator Smith, had supporting funds denied to them. This caused them to lose their re-elections, on the grounds that as POW/MIA advocates they got too close to information that would embarrass some politicians and some government "servants."  The Democrat Party did not have these problems, as I know of no Democrat member of either House who "went out on a limb" for the issue, except Congressman Murphy of Pennsylvania, who picked up the Missing Service Personnel Act after Congressman Rowland left Congress. Congressman Murphy left Congress "under a cloud." I firmly believe that his reintroducing the Missing Service Personnel Act helped color the cloud.

Bob was subpoenaed at a Congressional Hearing, and his statement was taken behind closed doors. (Again we must question the sense of having a "classified debriefing," since the Vietnamese knew everything Bob knew! Its real rationale was to keep the American public in the dark! His attorney at that hearing was Bill Bennett, who helped me write the Missing Service Personnel Act. Bill told me that while Bob was in the conference room for a long period of time, he had done very little testifying, as Congressman Solarz the Chairman of that Subcommittee, spent most of that time berating Bob. This was a pity because he could have learned a lot from him. The time was wasted. This is the same Congressman who President Clinton tried to make the ambassador to India, when his district, in New York City, was eradicated after the 1990 census. This Congressman had been one of the most proliferate users of unauthorized money drawn from the Congressional Bank (if you remember that scandal). At the time his security clearance was denied, I read a newspaper article that stated there were other reasons that caused the FBI to refuse him a security clearance. When I think of what that person is drawing in retirement pay, and that Bob has been robbed of his honor, life, and money due him, I become very angry. Bob shows more integrity in his everyday life today than most of the people I know, and many of the people I know are very honorable indeed. During the time Bob was a POW I believe that he did what he had to do to stay alive, and to return home. I have heard Bob talk about his situation, but in the entire time I have known him I have never heard him complain nor ask for sympathy. I do not believe that Bob could or would intentionally harm anyone. Bob Garwood's return did affect Congress in many ways. In my limited association with these disenfranchised Republicans, I have found that they all believe in Bob Garwood and still strongly support him. Senator Smith's opening statement to the Senate Select Committee on POW/MIA was "I believe Bobby Garwood!"

After the Senate Select Committee folded its disgraced hearing, and gave its badly flawed decision, Senator Bob Smith tried again. The senator was able to get Senatorial permission for a trip to Vietnam to check out some of the sites of live POW sightings. He had asked Bob Garwood to go with him, and promised him diplomatic immunity while he was in Vietnam. Such immunity is normal when a Senate or Congressional investigative trip is made. This allows all members of the group to be immune from arrest while in the foreign country. The concept of blanket immunity for staff members, and others accompanying the officials, is internationally recognized. Senator Smith applied for this immunity for all the people going on his junket, and it was approved. After it had already been approved by the Senate as a whole, Senator John McCain came "out of the woodwork" to demand that Garwood not be granted immunity, inferring "it would lower the esteem of the Senate to allow a Dishonorably Discharged veteran to go on a Senate-approved junket," and insisted that Bob Garwood's immunity be refused, so he couldn't go. This is one of the few times that Senator McCain publicly came out from behind his mask as a "POW Hero" and openly tried to disrupt an important POW/MIA effort. Senator McCain, coming in as late as he did to try to stop Garwood's immunity, caused many of the activists, who are well acquainted with McCain's reputation, to question if perhaps "his orders from Hanoi" were slow in arriving! The fact that Bob Garwood had freely agreed to travel to Vietnam, thus putting himself in great danger, to assist Senator Smith and ex-Congressman Hendon in their search for sites where Bob, and others, had reported seeing American POWs, did not matter to John McCain. No, the fact that Garwood's presence on the junket was the reason for the junket did not bother McCain's twisted sense of propriety. Senator Smith fought for Bob's immunity but finally it was denied. (I have been an observer of John McCain and the U.S. Senate for a good many years and I have been struck by McCain's ability to accomplish his personal desires, by demanding things others would be too embarrassed to try. I believe I have found the answer. The Senate is filled with old men, and old men are notoriously bothered by crying babies. Old men will often give such crying babies candy, just to shut them up, hence, McCain gets his way! Senator Smith disclosed to Garwood that diplomatic immunity for him had been denied, and suggested that he not travel to Vietnam. Senator Smith realized the physical danger Garwood would face by going back to a country he had deeply embarrassed, and undoubtedly still held a deep grudge against him. The Senator also recognized the mental strain that Garwood would be under, just by being back in Vietnam; without immunity it would be worse. But Garwood believed that learning the truth and proving the accuracy of his debriefing statements, was very important, so he agreed to go without immunity.

The junket traveled around Vietnam for several days, and Bob's statements all proved to be true. The compound at 17 Le Dee Street was exactly like he had said it was, and not as U.S. Intelligence had depicted it. The island he was taken to, where he had fixed a generator and had seen live Caucasians, had the buildings exactly where he said they were. Further investigation by Senator Smith and ex-Congressman Hendon also found the buildings where Bob had seen the Caucasians. They verified the inaccuracy of a U.S. intelligence report that the buildings had only recently had been built.

After the junket had been in Vietnam about a week, they were scheduled to go to a site where Garwood had seen several American POWs in the late 1970s (long after homecoming). The group was at the airport, loading on to helicopters for the trip when Garwood saw a person he recognized, and with whom he was personally acquainted. This person was a retired "Senior Colonel" in the Vietnamese Army. U.S. Intelligence had knowledge that this person existed but did not know his real name, nor did they have a picture of him. Garwood brought him to the attention of U.S. Intelligence immediately and verbally accosted the colonel, accusing him of murdering Captain Eisenbraun, and others. This colonel's duties had been to travel around all of the POW camps in South Vietnam, and North Vietnam. This colonel had life and death control over all prisoners. No prisoner could be systematically beaten or executed without his approval, and usually his presence. His reign of control went all the way back to when Veresace, Roraback, and Bennett were executed in 1965. After Garwood was pulled away from the colonel he was immediately taken into custody by the Vietnamese (no blows had been exchanged nor had the colonel been touched). It was "touch-and-go" for a while as no one knew what to expect as, "thanks to McCain," Garwood had no immunity and was strictly under Vietnamese jurisdiction. Garwood was confined to his hotel room for several days, but Senator Smith and ex-Congressman Hendon were finally able to get him released and out of the country. In retrospect, it is believed that the colonel was brought to the helicopter pick-up site expressly to raise Garwood's ire, and thus disrupt the purpose of the junket.

It is my belief that, hopefully in Bob's lifetime, he will be reinstated in the USMC, promoted to a senior non-commissioned officer rank, decorated, retired and paid in full for his service. If ever anyone deserved to be so honored it is Bob Garwood.

We must go back over a hundred years in history to 19th century France, to find a very good example of a person who was as badly mistreated by his government and eventually reinstated. Years after Captain Dreyfus, a Jewish officer in the French Army, had been brought to trial, and convicted on trumped-up charges, the French government admitted he was innocent. Senior members of the French Army General Command had wrongfully and intentionally convicted Captain Dreyfus on those false charges. He withered away on Devil's Island for many years, before the French government admitted he had been wrongfully convicted. Captain Dreyfus was eventually totally exonerated and restored to duty. Bob Garwood's anguish and punishment, FOR LIVING WHEN OTHERS WANTED HIM DEAD, has lasted nearly thirty years. Should we prevail and actually have a special prosecutor appointed to investigate the POW/MIA cover-up, part of the investigation should be a very close examination of the trials and tribulations Bob Garwood has suffered while a POW (during the war and the years he was held after the war), and with special emphasis with what he has suffered here at home since his return.

I shall wind up this chapter on Bob Garwood by telling how most other returned Vietnam POWs feel toward him. (The few ex-POWs who travel McCain's path are exempted from these accolades, as I believe most of them are hiding from a guilty conscience, or else they envy Garwood's tenacity.)

# CHAPTER SIX

# THE TIGHE TASK FORCE

**IN 1986,** THE THEN NEWLY-APPOINTED Director of the Defense Intelligence Agency, General Perroots, had an idea. He had heard so much about DIA incompetence that he wisely decided to appoint a Task Force to tell him what in the name of heaven was wrong, how it got that way and what could be done to fix it.

The Charter of Gen. Perroots was planned so that a report would be prepared by a task force of investigators, followed by a senior review panel, to review their work.

The Chairman would choose the task force members on the basis of integrity, excellence of knowledge of the intelligence process and knowledge of Vietnam. Lt. Gen. Eugene F. Tighe, Jr., USAF (Ret.), an excellent choice, was his man.

When Tighe filed his report on 27 May 1986 to Lieutenant General Leonard H. Perroots, USAF, he and his co-workers recommended that the entire report be made public. "My colleagues have asked that I note their unanimous support for the entire report; conclusions and recommendations."

The team consisted of: Eugene F. Tighe, Jr., Lieutenant General, USAF (Ret.), John B. Murray, Major General, USA (Ret.), Lester E. McGee, Jr., Colonel, USA (Ret.), Roberta Carper Maynard, John Francis McCreary, and Arthur G. Klos. When submitting the report, General Tighe added this comment:

> The intelligence indicates that American prisoners of war have been held continuously after Operation Homecoming and remain in captivity in Vietnam and Lao as late as 1989.

I have labored to explain our data and our technique because our findings disagree with those of the DIA. In conducting our investigation, we were shocked to find on page 3 of your package (VG-3 Return) that there is no category for a POW sighting—both for the DIA analysts and the Interagency Committee. We agree with the major findings of the report written by Col Kim Gaines, USAF, for Lt. Gen. Perroots, Director CIA in 1986. Copies of that report, known as the Gaines Report, are available.

General Perroots told the Senate Select Committee in August, 1992, "Vietnam can easily account for hundreds of Americans. They have not yet exercised their requisite will to do so."

As noted above, he was CIA Director in 1986.

## TECHNICAL ASSISTANCE

So that the Task Force would have the benefit of unquestioned technical support, Tighe asked that the director, DIA authorize outside expertise.

The rounded-out team then included:

> Polygraph: Dr. Chris Gugas, Ph.D., prominent polygraph expert. Director, "Professional Security Consultants," Los Angeles, Ca.

> Signal Intelligence: Maj. Gen. John Morrison, USAF (Ret.), Former Chief N.F.I.B., Signal committee.

> Vietnam Intelligence: Hoang Ly, former Chief of Vietnam Air Force intelligence and E.D.S. employee.

> Photo Interpretation: Mr. Dino Brugioni, skilled photo interpretation specialist. CIA (Ret.)

At the beginning of the report Tighe notes that he and his task force had spent hundreds of hours reviewing the files of the DIA PW/MIA Analysis Center over the previous weeks. They studied the manner in which the DIA officials and analysts handled the JCS directed mission to account for those American Military personnel missing in action.

Understanding the urgency and importance of reporting to the American people in general and the POW/MIA families in particular the known facts, Tighe makes a passionate appeal: "We believe . . . our insights . . . should be taken most seriously by you and the United States Government and that our recommendations be quickly implemented."

Tighe wrote a letter to the DIA dated 27 May 1986 to proposed members of a review panel requesting that they review his report.

> TO: Senior Review Panel
> Gen. Russell E. Dougherty, USAF (Ret.)
> Lt. Gen. John P. Flynn, USAF (Ret.)
> General Robert C. Kingston, USA (Ret.)
> Mr. Lyman Kirkpatrick
> Mr. H. Ross Perot
> Brig. Gen. Robinson Risner, USAF (Ret.)
> SUBJECT:   Tighe Task Force Review of DIA POW/MIA Analysis Center
>
> 1. Attached is the report of a lengthy and detailed examination of the files and activities of the DIA POW/MIA Analysis Center to determine whether or not it has met its obligations as regards analysis and evaluation of Intelligence since September 1981.
>
> 2. We ask that you review it, agree or disagree with the way it was conducted and its conclusions and recommendations and convey your judgments to the Director of the Defense Intelligence Agency, along with those of the Task Force. The findings are not all that important; the issue is vitally important. You are eminently qualified to

judge the necessity for action.

> (signed)
> Eugene F. Tighe, Jr.
> Lieutenant General, USAF
> (Ret., Chairman, enclosure a/s

The members of the Review Panel, after studying the report, informed General Perroots: "Lt. General Tighe asked that we serve as a Review Panel to go over the findings of his Task Force review of DIA's PW/MIA Analysis Center performance. We have completed our review of the report, support its conclusions and urge that you implement those of its recommendations that you have not already brought about, as quickly as possible. The findings of this report must not be forgotten. This issue, bringing American Military personnel home from Southeast Asia (dead or alive) as quickly as possible, must be acted upon with greatest vigor by all those U.S. Government officials responsible. We urge you to get on with support of the issue without delay."

## CONTENTS OF THE TIGHE REPORT

The report is rather long and is fairly liberal in the use of technical language. I have done my best to summarize it in layman's language as best I can. It is a sad story of a rather shocking lack of competence and lack of prioritization in the POW/MIA Issue, in spite of public declarations to the contrary. It does, however, have a very simple and constant theme running throughout the report: "The issue of whether Americans remain in Southeast Asia against their will, does NOT go away as long as there is evidence indicating their presence there." That statement was true the day it was written and remains true today.

Tighe discusses the origin of the report:

"General Perroots called me in to DIA for a lengthy discussion of this issue soon after he assumed his position as director of DIA on 1 October 1985. He was determined to assure a thoroughly professional DIA effort and asked for my help. " Tighe agreed to conduct an investigation at General Perroots' request because he believed there can be no more important government support for the U.S. fighting man than to return them to their loved ones. General Perroots gave Tighe his marching orders.

1.   "Review all of the current case files and handling of those files, looking for any indication of impropriety or "COVER-UP."

2.   "Evaluate the evidence regarding unaccounted for U.S. Military personnel in Southeast Asia and provide evaluation of DIA conclusions, and:

3.   "Focus on Live-Sighting reports in terms of quality of information, follow-up, intelligence collection, analysis and evaluation and disposition.

4.   "Recommend action as appropriate."

The director of DIA gave Tighe carte blanche to go anywhere his findings took him.

## THE GROWTH OF FRUSTRATION

So, eventually, the mission of the POW/MIA center at DIA changed from analyzing intelligence to "Resolving the Issue" by dong a fair amount of debunking the veracity of the intelligence, and raising the level of certainty of source bona fides at the expense of professionally analyzing the information. Skepticism replaced analyzing because the unit did not have the resources to analyze. They were overwhelmed with the amount of work in comparison with the size and resources of the unit. 'Prove it to me' became the dictum.

The impossible situation evolved that the POW family had to do the proving, not the people who were professionally trained and hired to do so by the DIA. General Tighe and his Task Force demonstrated extraordinary skill in their extraordinary contribution toward understanding the complex components of our war in Southeast Asia. They looked at the overall mission of the Defense Intelligence Agency and concluded that its top priority was and should continue to be that of furnishing intelligence on the Soviet Union, and the growing threat of terrorism and drugs and their interconnections. They found their task challenging because, given the inadequate resources available to the DIA to work on POW/MIA Issues, it was obvious that "Official high-level hyperbole from government officials may have distorted the true priority given to the POW/MIA Issue." In other words, the POW/MIA Issue became more of a political agenda in which the rhetoric outmatched the government's actual top priorities. Getting political support from veteran organizations was a higher priority than the amount of resources actually made available to the DIA unit that was tasked to explore all avenues possible in locating and recovering our POWs. Rhetoric was raising, among POW families, greater expectations than were attainable given the reality of resources dedicated to the issue. The politics of unattainable goals added a cruel edge to a highly emotional issue. The report made that very clear: "Therefore, the Task force concluded that the POW/MIA Issue should be removed from the DIA and a separate and permanent office established that focused only on POW/MIA matters. Such an office would have as its purpose a threefold task:

> 1. Assure priority in an organization which does not already have another priority one task (DIA must watch and analyze the USSR).
> 2. Assure a permanent, professionally built database concerning itself with the MIA of all wars.
> 3. Guarantee to last and perform professionally regardless of who occupies the White House, the Pentagon, or the Congressional Halls.

Then the Tighe report tells us that Americans have a right to charge the U.S. government with lying to them about the Government's real intentions:

> There may be a case in the court of public opinion, however, of culpable negligence attributable to the executive department at large, and to the totality of the myriad organizations involved in the PW/MIA Issue for their failure to

> ensure the highest priority in a final accounting.
> It must not be forgotten that the President said
> "the full resources of our government are now
> committed to these goals."

These words have to be devastating, even today, to POW families. The words mean that there never was and there is not an intention in the DIA to give priority to POWs/MIAs, not because they don't want to, but because, in spite of the campaign rhetoric, it never really was a high priority. The Gaines report that you read earlier also says that loud and clear. The interesting thing about the Tighe report is that it was ordered by and published by the DIA itself! To make a comparison, it is one thing for someone to tell you that the man you thought was your best friend does not even like you. In this case that is hearsay. But if the man whom you thought to be your best friend tells you himself, that is proof. So, it is one thing to have an agency outside the DIA tell you that the POW/MIA Issue is not a priority with them. But it is quite another thing for the DIA itself to tell you this. And remember that the Tighe report was reviewed, as you saw above, by primarily high ranking military, not, as McCain would say, a bunch of crazies. Their conclusion was, as we saw above: "We have completed our review of the report, support its conclusions and urge that you implement those of its recommendations that you have not already brought about, as quickly as possible."

They never were implemented.

If you are feint of heart, you may not want to read the rest of this chapter, for the remainder of the report is utterly devastating. I will quote the exact words of the report; otherwise you may think I was coming from some far left Think Tank.

During and since the Paris Peace Accords, Vietnam, the report says, the Vietnamese did the best they could to extract concessions from the United States. "Since the end of the war Vietnam has intended to use prisoners to extract maximal concessions from the U.S. Government . . . as one source put it, 'with a prisoner worth a factory, we judge that at some point bargains will be struck over live human beings.'"

The report goes on to say that what the government says is our publicly stated policy about prisoners of war and the missing in action "is not supported by the behavior of government organizations charged with carrying policy to effect . . . interagency cooperation is more apparent than real; collection priorities are among the lowest; claims on assets and monies are repeatedly denied in favor of routine agency operations."

How does one tell that to folks that believe the government is doing all that it can? How can we keep that from devastating POW families? We cannot.

All we can do is rally the troops to call on folks running for the Congress to declare what they will do about this situation once we elect them to office. If we fail to do that in 2008, then by the next election time comes around, most of us who have been the most deeply affected will no longer be able to rally the public to see to it that the men they elect today will fix the system tomorrow. If we remain silent for any reason, then we join the guilty. No political party; no allegiance to any powerful company; no allegiance to any particular interest groups excuses us from doing our duty. It may well be the last opportunity for the leading figures in the "movement" to act effectively.

The first thing Tighe's report noted was that the steadily growing number of reports (Live-Sighting Reports), which DIA received, the continual requests from media and public, and greater requirements to brief members of congress, etc., overwhelmed the POW/MIA unit.

Under those circumstances DIA personnel grew frustrated and depressed, "as a hostile Hanoi played cat and mouse with the U.S. public, releasing a few bodily remains of dead Americans to the U.S. from time to time."

So, eventually, the mission of the POW/MIA center at DIA changed from analyzing intelligence to "Resolving the Issue" by casting doubt on the veracity of the intelligence. This was done at the expense of professional analysis.

Skepticism was easier to handle than the hard work of analyzing. "Prove it to me" became the dictum, replacing "give me the information and I will study it." Imposing tasks on the shoulders of the providers of information replaced exercising the very talents for which they were hired by the DIA.

What Tighe found was ignorance, incompetence, and lack of imagination. His special investigation, headed by Col. Gaines, had discovered many of the faults this task force reports. "The files were of very inferior quality, and how the Congressional, inspector general, and intelligence community could have found them in acceptable shape was a mystery. . . . Overclassification, duplicate and triplicate papers, undated, unsigned and anonymously written memos abound. It was as if the incompetence of the communist bureaucracy was being challenged by American bureaucrats to finish last.

## DEMAND OUTSTRIPPED SUPPLY

The task force found that if the POW/MIA center of DIA was to make progress it had to do its job free from input from other agencies, especially in the evaluation of files and reports. In order for the POW/MIA unit to do its job properly it should not be involved in liaison with outside organizations That task "should be handled separately by other DIA and DOD elements."

The unit needed a variety and sufficiency of technical support to properly analyze the mass of data presently on hand and the backlog of intelligence not yet examined.

The slow pace of long delays in the investigation and the evaluation process caused by lack of typists was inexcusable.

The task force suggested that once this kind of technical support became part of the unit, then the retired data stored in Suitland, Maryland's Retired Records vaults be returned to the POW/MIA center. It can then be analyzed to see if it might contain information on POWs that had been missed.

## THE ANALYST'S APPROACH

The TTF noted that the prevailing practice and mind-set at the PM/MIA unit was one of doubt.

The adage, "Where there's Smoke there's Fire" was not

adopted. This mind-set was, even scientifically, the opposite of what any analyst is trained to do.

The fact that some reports were fabricated or less than accurate does not mean that all reports should be treated negatively. The reality was that the unit simply lacked a concept for working with unresolved cases except to tag them as fabrications.

The Center simply did not do its job.

## SINGLE SOURCE

The POW/MIA unit had the general practice of analyzing sighting information of live Americans in Indochina primarily in the form of briefs (KB's) from a single source, namely refugees interrogated by the Joint Casualty Resolution Center in Thailand. The report states that not enough attention was paid to information available from "CIA, Defense attaches, the Department of State, Joint volunteer agencies, the league of families, members of congress and concerned citizens and citizen groups."

The task force concluded that the "dearth of any other source reporting is puzzling at best."

As you may have noted, the list of lack of skills and the lack of real interest at the highest levels of government is so long that we can easily forget on one page what we wrote only 4 or 5 pages back. How all of this all could have happened in the most technologically advanced nation in the world, on an issue declared by our presidents as the most important national priority is "puzzling at best."

The task force concludes in this section that: "A review of the files gives a clear indication that the POW/MIA collection management activities has been, at best, undertaken on an ad-hoc basis resulting in a detrimental effect on the analytical efforts of the element. All evidence indicates that there has been no disciplined, coherent, all-source intelligence management plan or approach which actively engages the entire national intelligence community."

It was also pointed out that the POW/MIA center "provided

no evidence that it had investigated the Vietnamese penal system. It was a notable lack of knowledge, since an understanding of how the Vietnamese prison system works would be valuable in any attempt to find and locate POWs. The immense volume and complexity of their task should "have led management or analysts to seek the help of operations researchers, statisticians and methodologists." It did not.

## NO FOLLOW-UP OF SIGHTINGS

The task force explained that the reason they had spent so much time in their report on the quality of the unit's analysis work was the fact that there were known eyewitness sightings with various dates of information that had not been followed up on with proper analysis. This included "sightings in Laos wherein the non-Asians are engaged in economic activity, plowing, mining or construction and under Vietnamese control."

Therefore it was clear that the unit's work did not "begin to approach the substantive analytical issues, much less exhaust the potential intelligence value of the sighting reports. . . . Our review has uncovered a repeated pattern of premature mental closure. The files show a tendency by the analyst to make up his mind about the value of a report before his own inquiries are satisfied." And, once again, the task force concluded that the work done in the unit "was heavily influenced by a bias that all refugee reports are suspect unless proven otherwise." And then the task force made this devastating conclusion: "Consequently, the credibility of POW/MIA Center's judgment that a refugee account is a fabrication must be considered low. . . A lack of basic evidentiary skills is illustrated plainly in the POW/MIA Center's failure to analyze the substance of a report. . . Evidently the analysts have no criteria for judging the probity or credibility of information, independent of its source. The files reflect few judgments about clarity, specificity, or amounts of details. These are basic evidentiary tasks . . . . As for DIA itself, there are serious indications that at best it has not fulfilled its promise to congressional oversight committees that it "vigorously pursues each and every report which could help resolve these issues"

There is much more in the report of great interest, but I will conclude here with the Task Force analysis of the quality of sightings that the POW/MIA unit discounted as unreliable. "The assertion that sources easily distinguish Americans is not supported by evidence. The POW/MIA Special Office has several cases in which an individual, later proven to be Eurasian, French or other non-American was identified by several sources as an American. We are not alone in reaching our findings. In 1983 and 1984 testimonies before Congress, both Admiral Paulson and General Williams testified that 92 to 97 percent of the refugee accounts were truthful. . . . It establishes a probability and a presumption that at least 92 of every 100 refugee sightings will be truthful, regardless of motive or other circumstance."

Once again let me reiterate that seasoned military men and experts, not wild-eyed hippies compiled this report. It tells, as does the Gaines report and other reports, the very sad story of neglect, incompetence, lack of resources and dedication to what we all agree is a national priority. It is a frightening tale relative to our present concerns about terrorism. That is why it is our belief that we should pause during the 2008 election season and do what needs to be done, i.e., bring the POW/MIA Issue to the public forefront once again, as we did in the past. This time, instead of testifying by word, let us testify by political action. Let it be our publicly announced policy that no one gets our vote who does not publicly declare that they will see to it that what happened to our POWs and their families will never happen to our children and our grandchildren. If we do not do this then all our public statements will not erase the fact that we are part of the problem rather than part of the solution. A nation that does not vote its needs ends up without them.

## WHITE HOUSE REACTION

One can only imagine the consternation, confusion, the hasty back room meetings, and the panic that followed the reading of the Tighe Report by NSC Asian Affairs Director Dick Childress.

He initiates the cover-up, the enormous attempts by the White House to deride, ridicule, and destroy the report's conclusions. As if in total desperation he cries out: The report "has the most serious consequences." He directed Tighe's boss, Lt. Gen. Leonard Perroots, to nullify the report before the public became aware of it. In his book, *An Enormous Crime* (by former Congressman Bill Hendon and Beth Stewart, St. Martin's Press, 2007), former Congressman Bill Hendon relates how Perroots called him and said that "the policy people have told me this is too hot and have directed me to scrub the report before it is released." Regretfully, Hendon tells us that Perroots cooperated with the cover-up by: 1. Pretending that the American POWs mentioned as alive in the Tighe Report were, in fact, deserters. 2. Discrediting the human intelligence in the report that was described as credible. 3. Attempting to force the members of the Tighe Report to deny their own painstakingly accurate assessments and conclusions. Hendon had already been informed by a Secret Service agent that what the White House was saying publicly, i.e. that there were no POWs remaining in Vietnam, was a lie. He told Hendon that as far back as 1981 he overheard a conversation emanating from the Oval Office that said exactly the contrary. CIA Director William Casey met with Hendon on October 7, 1986, and tried to pressure him to stop talking about the subject publicly. And, in a moment of angry candor he said to Hendon. "Look, the nation knows they are here, everybody knows they're there. You guys have written the President, you're always talking about it, Gene Tighe is always talking about it, but there's no groundswell of support for getting the men out." Shame on Perroots, shame on William Casey, and his superiors in the White House. Shame on them all.

Fr. Patrick Bascio is a retired Roman Catholic priest, lecturer and writer with a doctorate and two master's degrees in an array of social science fields. He has worked internationally on human rights campaigns and has been the Economic Advisor to the Prime Minister of Grenada and that country's representative and Counselor to various United Nations committees. In addition, he is the Former Director of the Salve Regina University Master's Program in Humanities and the Founder and Director of the Ph.D. Program. His teaching duties have included the University of the West Indies (Port of Spain, Trinidad) and Umbwe College (Mount Kilimanjaro, Tanzania). His publications include *The UN Was My Parish* (1979), *Building a Just Society* (1981), *The Failure of White Theology: A Black Theological Perspective* (1994), and *Gorbachev and the Collapse of the Soviet Communist Party* (1994), with co-author Evgueny Novikov, former member of Soviet Central Committee and high-level defector.

# CHAPTER SEVEN

# THE GAINES REPORT

**A TASK FORCE COMPRISING FIVE MEMBERS** was assembled on 20 February 1992 headed up by Colonel Kimball M. Gaines. Its assignment was "to conduct a hardnosed objective examination of POW/MIA substantive issues and procedures and to report findings and recommendations to the Director within thirty days." They were also instructed to have discussions with supervisory and working level personnel within the POW Committee Staff and with the National Security Agency Representative to DOD, and were to check "all active first-hand-live-sighting case files" and had access to a number of previously closed cases.

## THE DATABASE

The database of POW/MIA sightings and information is described in the report as "a wasteland, neither structured nor maintained to support analysts adequately in all areas." Only one technician was responsible for database maintenance and she had to work with an outmoded file system. In addition she was dealing with far more material than she could competently handle. And, since the database, its structure, maintenance, design, and upgrade is absolutely essential, the central foundation for keeping track of the DIA PW program, "why a recognized problem of such importance . . . had gone unsolved simply boggles the mind." The report points out that since the database was not properly taken care of in term of equipment and sufficient personnel, the Task Force "does not have complete confidence in the conclusions resulting from the POW Division analytic process." So, we had one person using outmoded equipment all by herself to keep track of one of the most important matters to the nation, a matter close to the heart of every American. Such negligence, such dereliction of duty is incomprehensible. The person or persons responsible for this travesty need to come forth or be brought forth and, at a minimum, never again hold a job in the United States government. Once again, there must be no statute of limitations on firing a person or persons responsible for this dishonorable handling of a national treasure of such enormous and personal meaning to millions of Americans. Further, the report tells us that, "The existence of shoddy case-files is not new and others have pointed this out, the latest official mention being a flag-rank memo to VO as late as Sept. 1985." And was anything done about the problem after it had been pointed out by such a high ranking person in 1985? Not really.

## THE COLLECTION EFFORT

What about collecting intelligence for the database? Was the Task Force satisfied with that? Here is what they wrote: "Outside the mainstream, is the only way to describe the collection effort, and one telling proof of the pudding is the fact that it took out-siders . . . .to raise the priority of collection from five to three in the National Intelligence Topics (NITS). None of this initiative originated from the POW/MIA Division." Once again, we see in-comprehensible negligence, and mismanagement of such enor-mous consequences to POW lives and those of their families. These lives were torn apart, shredded, abused and neglected by the very agency and men to whom those lives were solemnly en-trusted. Members of the Task Force were told by the employees that we do not employ enough analysts. "There is somehow never enough time for it because of 'other priorities' although they think it would be a really good thing to do if they could." These are the words of the folks in the agency itself, words that accuse and con-demn the superiors who did not provide sufficient personnel for a task the President proudly and solemnly declared to be of the highest national interest. And then the report tells us this startling information: "In fact, the Chief of the Analysis Branch feels that there is probably enough information on hand already to allow a definitive judgment on the live POW Issue in North Vietnam, but they just can't get around to doing it." And as if this is not mind-boggling enough, the Task Force reports this totally damning fact: "It should be noted with trepidation that there are some 600 hearsay reports of live sightings backlogged in the Division which have not had any evaluation." Many live sightings had been reported. Take, for example the ones at Thach Ba Lake, where three on-site investigations took place in 1992-93.

DOD concluded that the sightings were fabrications, because the buildings described by the eyewitness did not exist.

And yet, a few months later, Senator Bob Smith traveled to the location and found the buildings, exactly as described by the source in the report. Smith then visited two other sites that had been discredited by our government. Both turned out, once again, accurate. What did McCain and Kerry do about all of this?

They simply say in their report at the conclusion of their Committee's work that there was no evidence that any American POWs were alive. They should resign.

They sat there day after day hearing testimony that many of our men still languished in East Asian prisons and treated that information as if it did not exist. The voices of at least two of the other Senators, Smith and Grassley, on the Senate Select Committee were ignored and, by neglect, suppressed. The Committee itself contradicted it own evidence. "The Committee repeatedly requested that DOD again conduct a full review of returnee debriefings. DOD declined to do so. The Committee Chairman and Vice Chairman were allowed access to the debriefings, but the volume precluded more than a sampling."  Kerry and McCain were nationally prominent Senators and could have protested publicly and strongly at the DOD's insensitivity to POW/MIA families, but they did not. The Committee repeatedly asked the DOD to conduct a full review of returnee debriefings. They were turned down. The Committee then requested that the Committee staff be allowed to review previous debriefings. DOD once again denied access. The report says simply: "Therefore, the Committee has placed into the Archives the computer listings of the debriefing results and encourages the public to review these comments and draw their own conclusions."

## REVAMPING NEEDED

The report correctly assesses the situation. "The ultimate bottom line to this entire review is the absence of leadership. Every condition uncovered and detailed in this report attests to that fact. This Division is not an organized effort and it is certainly not a model that deserves emulation. . . ." Conditions were so bad that the Task Force came to the conclusion that the POW/MIA Division could not provide the Director, DIA with the level and quality of support needed to get the job done. McCain and Kerry, in spite of this clear and damning evidence praised DIA for the great work they did. Since they are neither naïve nor stupid, the reader can join the rest of us in determining their motivation for such a ridiculous conclusion.

## INITIAL RECOMMENDATIONS

The Task Force recommended that the revamping of the DIA would demand: A white paper, regular press summaries, cultivation of "friendly" journalists, work with the League of Families, respond, on a selective basis, to misinformation disseminated in the public forum, actively Involve the entire National Intelligence Apparatus, make Interagency Intelligence Action Group work, increase DCID (Director of Central Intelligence Directives) priority from three to two, involve other U.S. agencies  the investigative effort, and improve the DIA POW/MIA effort by implementing the recommendations of the Task Force.

## CONDITION OF CASE FILES

It was the finding of the Task Force that case files were not complete and, in some cases, not well-maintained, that there was no centralized log of incoming reports, that individual reports containing information on different cases were often not reproduced and placed in a coordinated way with other relevant case files, that cases were resolved by making judgments on material, and that when asked about this the analysts admitted that there was no documentation in the file to support that reasoning. Polygraph records were not kept in case files where they belonged and details of the polygraph exam were not filed. Nor could a resume of the case stating its status, together with an explanation of the conclusion in "clear and lucid exposition" be found in many cases. Also there were many cases that contained loose papers and undated scribbled analyst notes. The Task Force wrote: "There is no centralized suspense system to ensure tracking of requests for reinterview, polygraph requests, attempts to locate refugees, and attempts to locate related information. (For example: there are numerous cases in which follow-up action was not completed for several months or a few years.)"

## DEBUNKING

The report comes out swinging. It declares that there is a dangerous mindset of debunking good POW/MIA news. There is an abundance of evidence of this mindset. In early 1991, Colonel Millard Peck, head of the Pentagon's POW/MIA office resigned in disgust after only eight months on the job. His departure statement was electrifying. He said, "The mind-set to 'debunk' is alive and well. It is held at all levels. . . . Practically all analysis is directed to finding fault with the source. Rarely has there been any effective, active follow-through on any of the sightings. . . . The sad fact is that . . . a cover-up may be in progress. The entire charade does not appear to be an honest effort and may never have been." He also said, "From what I have witnessed, it appears that any soldier left in Vietnam, even inadvertently was, in fact abandoned years ago, and that the farce that is being played is no more than political sleight of hands done with "smoke and mirrors" to stall the issue until it dies a natural death." This became a permanent mindset, one that became over time an investigative technique that focused on veracity of sources with a view toward discrediting them. The mind set deepened as promising reports turned out to be fabrications. The report states, "Unfortunately, the mindset now permeates the Division in other than investigative matters, and it appeared during the review period that just about any new idea on the POW/MIA Issue is met with a negative response." The Task Force then makes a very important observation, i.e., that even more unfortunate in this entire situation is the fact that the mindset has become so ordinary that the analysts involved "are not even consciously aware of their negative approach." Nor is it a new problem. Admiral Tuttle, former supervisor, complained of the same problem in 1981 and, although he tried, he did not succeed in changing the conditions. Those who report sightings of POWs, especially, those who are already settled in the United States would have no ulterior motives for reporting the sightings and they should be taken seriously. What the Task 'Force discovered is that rather than welcoming those who reported sightings to the government, those who came forth with information were "badgered when they come forward." The result of such badgering is that "word gets around the refugee community and information dries up." People looking on at such a condition must wonder, what in the name of heaven is wrong with American public servants? What is the huge American bureaucracy doing all day long? What are hundreds of Congressmen and senators doing all day long? It is shameful. What a disappointment to those who look to America as a bright city sitting on top of the hill. The Task Force's recommendation: In other words, plan, organize, direct, control, and coordinate. The report points out that by their own admission the DIA leadership is not only flawed, but does not even manage! All aspects of ADP are deficient . . . analysts have not been given the requisite six week DIA Training Program . . . There are no enumerated goals or objectives upon which any direction is based. Functions are carried out on an ad hoc basis. . . . During this review one GS-14 was humiliated by a Congressman, who terminated the session by throwing the former's papers on the floor and verbally admonishing him. . . ."

And read this: "As a general comment, most of the discrepancies in the POW Division can be traced to this lack-of-management as well as a strongly entrenched attitude that they can do no wrong, even in the face of evidence to the contrary. This attitude has also been abetted by the Congressional review of May 1983 through June 1984 and the DO review of March 1985, both of which essentially white-washed the whole operation.

My God! In other words, from the work rooms of the DIA to the Halls of Congress, the system is a mess, totally broken down. And yet McCain and Kerry, after hearing all this testimony and much, much more, had the gall to insist at that time and continue to strongly insist today that after careful study the "Committee concluded that there are no POWs unaccounted for!"

## NO OVERSIGHT

The Task Force discovered that the Division opened, investigated, analyzed, and closed cases without the benefit of review by anyone else to validate its findings. This entire operation, important as it was to the honor and integrity of an entire nation was not reviewed by objective outside inspectors. A backlog of approximately 600 hearsay live sighting reports had accumulated at the time of the Task Force report and nothing was done to eliminate this shortfall.

But there was no shortfall of cover-up. In his 12 March 1986 testimony to Congress, the Division Director stated: "No budgetary constraints are imposed on research, interviews and investigative follow-up associated with DIA's pursuit of POW/MIA information."

The Director succeeded in his ruse to give the impression that the DIA was dedicated and competent in its efforts to find POWs. Not only is it not competent but DIA analysts have no credentials for the work they do and are not trained investigators.

In other words for America's highest priority the investigators are not even trained investigators; the case files, the Task Force discovered, are neither investigated nor professionally analyzed.

## EXPLOITING REFUGEES

As acknowledged by the CIA during Task Force coordination, DOD has a wealth of background and expertise on refugee screening and exploitation (e.g. Soviet emigrés, Cuban emigrés, etc.) Coordination needs to be effected with JCRC (Joint Casualty

Resolution Center) to ensure that this expertise is being brought to bear on the problem of exploitation. Other matters need to be covered with JCRC. For example, the POW/MIA Division perceived JCRC's charter as limited to background questions to refugees concerning "sightings." Their concern is that more detailed exploitation will be adversely regarded by the host government, and JCRC could lose its charter. This is naive. Once the host government allows access to the refugee assuredly it considers that exploitation will be complete. There have been detrimental effects from this conservative policy, namely, in-depth questions did not get directed to sources; sources disappear before being reinterviewed, as they move on through the refugee stream; and essential information on other than live sightings is not collected.

## TASK FORCE RECOMMENDATIONS

The report recommended that : "(1) VO-PW should launch a massive 90-day review of the system and establish a professional collection posture under the supervision of an expert in all-source collection, prepare an all-source collection plan, introduce and validate a separate POW/MIA NSRL, review all relevant VO-PW analysts, collectors, and supervisors to ensure that the selection effort is managed dynamically and aggressively. (2) The Collection and Analysis functions should be divided between separate branches of the Division, in order to give visibility and a more separate identity to this crucial function.

## EXAMINE THE INTERNAL WORKINGS OF THE DIVISION

The report recommended also that each branch of VO-PW be headed by a GS-14 who has considerable analytical and/or operational responsibilities in addition to the supervisory and managerial responsibilities required of a branch chief. They also recommended that since supervisors, because of personnel shortages, were involved in analytical, collection, or operational responsibilities "other than SUPERVISING and MANAGING activities of their branches," management duties were often overlooked. In other words leave it to the experts to exercise their expertise. There should be a clear distinction between analysis, collection, and investigation. Fudging the differences produces shoddy work in each area.

Too much time is spent by analysts in telephone interviews with sources. Investigative activities consume an inordinate amount of time that should be spent on analysis and/or collection. In this regard, VO-PW requires its own limited collection and interview capability for selected sources of information as active collectors and interviewers is important to the operation of the office. The Task Force points out that this makes it very important that administrative and clerical support to VO-PW is provided, and that the lack of such support was a major shortcoming. A newly-hired secretary at that time was quickly becoming proficient in supporting the Division but was completely overloaded by typing demands. At the time of the Task Force's review of VO-PW, there were at least 48 finished reports, 25 collection emphasis messages, and 11 case evaluations along with a two-inch stack of other items awaiting typing. For several days, nothing except material for the Director's upcoming Congressional testimony was typed. A major backlog exists in two areas: final evaluations of sighting reports and filing of data on the Vietnamese prison/reeducation camp system. Also, there were 179 resolved first-hand sighting cases for which the analyst has written an evaluation, but the evaluations were awaiting editing and typing. Some of these dated back to 1981. Also, there were at the time of the Task Force report, "approximately 60 unresolved live sighting cases of Americans in a POW-type environment." Another area of shocking incompetence discovered by the Task Force was that specific knowledge on the prison/reeducation camp system and over one hundred reports had been received, some with information on several camps. These reports have been read but never filed in the appropriate camp folder. In addition, unbelievably, the office had a minimal system of keeping track of taskings. There did not appear to be a clear system of logging incoming requirements (suspended or open-ended), assigning them to an individual for action, and tracking their completion. "A single Air Force Master Sergeant serves as administrative NCO, but her many other duties and the lack of any other administrative personnel serves to make administration within VO-PW an ad hoc affair."

## IMPORTANCE OF PLACE

The Task Force wisely insisted that the POW/MIA Division "rank" of place within the DIA would signal its importance or lack of it within the DIA. Also, "many requests requiring POW/MIA Division action are high-priority requiring rapid response and should not be slowed by layers of bureaucracy . . . the position of the Division determines the "clout" it will have within and outside the Agency." The Task Force report pointed out that the fact that this had not been a consideration in the past encouraged other agencies to not take seriously its vital and emotionally important work. The interest in finding and rescuing POWs/MIAs was so low that "In previous years, the POW/MIA Division was reduced to five personnel, and Division personnel state that a previous Director "planned to close us up." This is prima facie evidence that the "DIA does not place high priority on the POW/MIA Issue." This was the case, in spite of the solemn and loud declarations made by presidents, senators, and congressmen, especially during election seasons. Those members of the Senate Select Committee that heard all this testimony, who voted to close down the Committee because "there was no credible evidence that any POW/MIAs still lived in captivity" have a lot to answer for. Unfortunately, there were in that Committee those who disagreed with McCain and Kerry, but they all voted, in the end, as a sign of unity, to declare the Committee's work finished. It was unity in perfidy.

# CHAPTER EIGHT

# U.S. POWS, KOREA & RUSSIA

ON NOVEMBER 10, 1992, the Committee received testimony from Dr. Paul M. Cole, an analyst with the International Policy Department of the RAND Corporation. RAND has undertaken a project through the National Defense Research Institute. Originally, the project was to review information concerning the fate of American POW/MIAs in Korea. In April, 1992, the project was expanded to include any American servicemen that had been taken to the Soviet Union or its allies during World War II, the early Cold War, or the Korean War. Interestingly enough what had previously been considered a difficult subject with very few clues, Cole discovered that the record of Korean MIA/POW cases was abundant and even organized chronologically and geographically before being reorganized alphabetically. So optimistic was Cole that he testified to the Committee that once the original chronological and geographic databases were recreated few questions would remain unanswered. He estimated that more than 2000 Korean POWs who made it alive to a camp, but were not repatriated, are known as POW/BNR (Body Not Recovered). The location and number of more than 2,000 POW/BNR remains can be estimated with great certainty, although what happened to them in the meantime could not be known. Those who did not make it to the camps should not be listed as POWs, because there is too much uncertainty about them. As many as 3,500 MIAs have likely died without any derivation. Where, when or how may never be known because the U.S. has not been able to determine where they died. On the other hand, about 900 burial sites were provided to the United States by the North Koreans, but no names were associated with particular remains. It is also possible that many POWs were sent to China from North Korea for interrogation but Cole concluded that there is no evidence that any of them were detained in China against their will. What evidence we received from POWs focused on Russian interrogators. But Cole felt that there was no hard evidence that any of the POWs were transferred to the Soviet Union for interrogation. But a very interesting incident occurred in Moscow that also throws caution on the other side, i.e., should make us cautious not to ensure that American prisoners were not brought to Russia for interrogation. The incident was that the Russians handed over to Ambassador Toon and to Cole documents, the contents of which described the manner in which the documents could be either, changed, distorted, or otherwise disposed in order to keep the truth from anybody who might discover them. In other words, the documents handed over by the Russians to the Americans themselves contained evidence that the Russians were not telling the truth! Somebody in Russia goofed on that one. In any case, Cole concluded that the amount of U.S. POWs who might have been transferred to Soviet or Chinese territory would be less than 100. He also mentioned that the review of POW/MIA Issues conducted by the RAND Corporation issues related to the Korean War was flawed because of inaccuracies of the data they originally gathered. Information or lack of it continued to fluctuate because of "contradictory, ambiguous, inconsistent, or a mixture of any of these."

In 1991, the Department of Defense informed Congress that 389 POWs in North Korea had not been repatriated or accounted for by the Korean People's Army and the Chinese. However, Cole notes that of those 389 MIAs, 180 may or may not have ever been prisoners, and there is one case which has in fact been resolved. There is no evidence in many cases that those listed as POWs were ever seen alive. When one considers the conditions under which POWS lived and the harsh treatment they received, "the likelihood of survival for this group was very low."

It is not a bit surprising that the Soviet military spent a good deal of time in North Korea during the war or that some U.S. POWS and Army personnel have informed military intelligence that they had been questioned by Russian officers in North Korea or China. Victor Alexandrovich Bushuyev, Deputy Chief of Intelligence for the 64th Soviet Air Corps told Cole on September 16, 1992, "We had contacts with the American POWs, mainly the pilots. We weren't interested in anybody else. I was responsible for organizing the interrogations and for processing all of the information received during the interrogations."

It is well-documented and not at all surprising, given their "comradely relationship" that Soviet troops and technicians lived and worked in North Korea during the war. Returning POWS reported having been questioned by Russian interrogators in both North Korea and China. Dr. Cole quotes a 1974 description of interrogations of U.S. POWS in Korea. Interrogations were carried out by Russians, Chinese and North Koreans, but mostly by the Chinese. The dominance of Chinese presence occurred after they made their incursion South in October of 1950 so to come to the aid of the North Korean government. The preponderance of interrogators were Chinese. They took over the responsibility for POWs from the Koreans. This action caused a rift between the North Koreans and the Chinese that lasted throughout the conflict, because the North Koreans only reluctantly gave up this responsibility.

POWs reported that tense feelings concerning who was to have custody of a new POW often erupted, leading to bad feelings. Not infrequently, POWs reported that they were captured by North Koreans and turned over to the Chinese only after much heated discussion and sometimes near violence between the two groups.

In some cases, a POW remained in North Korean custody for prolonged periods of time.

Gen. Loettke told the Committee during his testimony that the effort to reach conclusions has been complicated by the official deceptions that characterize Soviet history: "They have lied to us, and they have said openly that they have lied to us. So we know if you develop that historically, they did keep some Americans in World War II, men they picked up in German POW camps as the Allies moved in."

As regards POWS in Korea, the Russians have already admitted that they interrogated U.S. POWs during the Korean War. The only question that remains is, did the interrogations take place in North Korea, near the Chinese border, or within the borders of the Soviet Union, or in both places? General Loeffke testified that he questioned a Russian Colonel, and "at the end of an hour and a half I asked if I could record this on tape, and we did, and he on tape said yes, I interrogated American POWs in Russian uniform.

And he did it more than once.

And he said his colleagues did it, too. . . ." The Colonel mentioned a specific base which is located in Russia.

In May, 1992, Al Graham, a Committee investigator, was sent to Moscow to study the entire issue of Americans having been interrogated by Russians during the Korean conflict. He conducted interviews with Russian officials, citizens, and retired officers who served in Southeast Asia and Korea.

At Committee hearings on November 10, 1992, he told the Committee that Soviet military officers interrogated some U.S. POWs during the Korean War, some of them probably on Soviet territory. He also mentioned, however, that, probably under pressure from higher-ups, later changed their stories. One in particular was a famous Russian colonel who also happened to be a Far East expert who was stationed at Khabarovsk from 1950 to 1954. This individual was asked by the chief of the general staff to review all documents on Korea.

At first he said that Soviet military interrogated some American servicemen in Korea, and that others were selected for transfer to the U.S.S.R. for the same purpose, at a naval base called Posyet. This base served as a transit point for the movement of literally hundreds of Americans north to Khabarovsk. He was unable to say what happened to the Americans after the interrogations were completed. He himself had interrogated two Americans, one of them a Lieutenant Colonel Black. He also admitted interrogating two American POWs in North Korea, and that he was but one of between 10 to 25 Soviet interrogators involved in this process.

By his own admission on September 29, 1992, in the presence

of General Loeffke, he said he had received a phone call from the Foreign Intelligence Service the night before he changed his story. Since to have admitted to the United States that the Soviets handled American servicemen illegally, no doubt to get military secrets, could have caused a diplomatic firestorm, it was understandable that the word got out not to be too specific to investigator Graham.

So, Mr. Graham's conclusion was that: "Although we have no direct evidence to prove it, there appears to be a strong possibility that at least a handful of U.S. POWs, possibly more, were transferred to Soviet territory during the Korean War."

Therefore, it remains possible that one or more could still be alive and that the Russians would never admit that this is true because of the very severe diplomatic consequences that would follow. Unfortunately, several presidents of the United States, even if they have ample evidence that Americans remained and remain, have taken the same position as the Russians, i.e., leave it alone.

## COLONEL CORSO

Colonel Phillip Corso (U.S. Army Ret.), now deceased also testified on this subject. Corso, as we have mentioned earlier, was a former National Security Aide and POW specialist to President Eisenhower. Col. Corso was present during the exchange of prisoners at Panmunjom in Korea at the end of the war. Incredibly, his previous attempts to tell our government about what happened to Americans there were ignored. Corso: "Five hundred of our prisoners, our estimate was, were not returned that we knew were sick and wounded and seriously ill or wounded and will not survive unless they are brought back soon for treatment. As we had our staff meetings with the chief of staff and so forth I was briefed on the subject. I would brief my superiors on this and then the position was to compile this information in the form to send to Washington, to the Pentagon. *Nothing was done in the Far East with this information.*"

## HEARD BUT NOT SEEN

Russians interrogators had a unique experience in that neither they nor the translators they employed ever saw any of the POWs with their own eyes. They were prohibited from seeing the Americans. The Main Intelligence Directorate in Moscow would give us questionnaires: ask this, ask that, whatever we thought was interesting. They would enter the building from a different side before the POWs were brought there, and proceed to the room where the interrogations would be held. They would just sit there quietly until the prisoners were brought in. They were all in the same room but the prisoners were separated from the Russians by a thin wooden wall. So they had no visual contact. The translators sat with the Russians, so there was no problem hearing the questions. The answers were immediately translated by the interpreters.

Only then would they bring in the POWs. "We would sit behind the wall, a thin wooden wall, and the translators would sit with us. We heard everything." The interrogations were in English, or course. The Russians had no interest in bringing the Americans to Russia. The only information the Russians were interested in was easily obtainable on Korean soil. This way there would be no diplomatic problems down the line with the Americans.

In any case, Russian counterintelligence had little interest in the Americans. The questioning was more or less routine. They already had the planes and the parts to study.

The Russians were prepared to grant political asylum should someone ask for it. The Russians involved in these interrogations estimate that they dealt with several hundred pilots. Practically all of the American POWs belonged to the Chinese.

The Korean War was conducted not by the Koreans but by the Chinese and Soviets.

The Koreans, for the most part, took care of the menial tasks, like loading and unloading vehicles or trains and building roads. This picture of the interrogation situation was confirmed in the testimony of G. Korotkov, who participated in interrogations of

American POWs from the Korean War period: "Interrogations were conducted in an especially equipped site at a junction of the Korean, Chinese and Soviet borders. So far we have been unable to determine the exact location of this site. The Soviet side was not engaged in transporting American POWs to this site. Probably they were brought by Korean servicemen, who then took them away after interrogations."

Did any American POW/MIA die in the Soviet Union?

Dr. Cole interviewed two Soviet military advisers in Korea who had contact with two American POWs. One, First Lieutenant Niemann was seen by a reliable source. Niemann was listed on the RAND and TFR lists as dead.

Another Soviet military adviser recalled having contact with "Lt. Colonel V. Black" in order to arrange an interview with Pravda. A George Blake, of California, has not been accounted for since he was shot down in May 1951. He was reported seen alive by a U.S. POW in Pyongyang in March 1952.

George Blake may be the "V. Black" who was identified in the *Pravda* article and seen by the Soviet military adviser.

Soviet intelligence wanted to recruit agents. Blake's decision to work for the KGB, if that is what actually happened, certainly would be welcomed by the KGB. No one is going to look a gift horse in the mouth.

There is no evidence that the North Koreans or the Chinese had any interest in recruiting agents. But, as we have already seen, any listing of a POW by the DIA is suspect, given the sloppy and outrageous manner in which all documents were handled by the DIA, and the cavalier manner in which POW/MIA personnel were recorded as deceased. In the early and mid-1950's, according to Dr. Cole, the U.S. government did not deny that some Americans may have been transported from Korea or China to the territory of the USSR.

For example, according to press reports, in May 1954, the U.S. State Department passed a note to the Soviets accusing them of having transferred American prisoners to the Soviet Union from Korea. The subject never became a big issue in American/Soviet relations.

A document of February 4, 1954 of Interior Minister Sergei Krughemseves indicates that six American citizens were being held in special prisons and camps of the Ministry of Internal Affairs. It was top secret, and was purely for the use of the Interior Ministry.

## THE CHINA FACTOR

Former POW Sgt. Steve E. Kiba testified that some of our POWS were transferred to the People's Republic of China (PRC). This is not speculation on his part, because he was one of them. Sgt. Kiba, an Air Force radioman, was interned in China for 32 months after his capture on January 12, 1953 as a POW during the Korean War, and remained there until his release on August 4, 1955. He described what it was like. As Sgt. Kiba testified: "They were sadistic and barbaric . . . threatened me with all kind of horrendous tortures, and they even did some of them. . . . They told me I would never go home unless I cooperated. And they threatened to keep me for life. And they kept some of my friends for life. They're still there."

Kiba testified that American POWs were abandoned after the 1953 ceasefire, and some of them never returned. He saw ten to fifteen Caucasians during his stay. He testified: "It is a known fact that we abandoned American servicemen after [World War II, Korea and Vietnam] and let their families down. I know we abandoned some because I saw some of them."

President Eisenhower abandoned American POWs after the Korean War in North Korea, Red China and the Soviet Union, and admitted this in a press conference on April 29, 1959. Eisenhower acknowledged that not all American POWs were repatriated after the Korean War ceasefire.

## DOLORES ALFOND

The testimony of Dolores Apodaca Alfond, national chairperson of the National Alliance of Families for the return of America's Missing Servicemen, before the Senate select committee, on Nov. 11, 1992, was revealing. Her pilot brother, Capt. Victor J. Apodaca, out of the Air Force Academy, was shot down over Dong Hoi, North Vietnam, in the early evening of June 8, 1967. At least one person in the two-man plane survived. Beeps from a pilot's distress radio were picked up by overhead helicopters, but the cloud cover was too heavy to go in.

Hanoi has recently turned over some bone fragments that are supposed to be Apodaca. The Pentagon first declared the fragments to be animal bones. Now it is telling the family—verbally—that they came from the pilot. But the Pentagon, for unexplained reasons, will not put this in writing, which means Apodaca is still unaccounted for. Also the Pentagon refuses to give Alfond a sample of the fragments so she can have testing done by an independent laboratory. She pleaded with the committee not to shut down in two months, as scheduled. Also, she was critical of the committee, and in particular Kerry and McCain, for having "discredited the overhead satellite symbol pictures, arguing there is no way to be sure that the [distress] symbols were made by U.S. POWs." She also criticized them for similarly discounting data from special sensors, shaped like a large spike with an electronic pod and an antenna, that were airdropped to stick in the ground along the Ho Chi Minh Trail. These devices served as motion detectors, picking up passing convoys and other military movements, but they also had rescue capabilities. Specifically, someone on the ground—a downed airman or a prisoner on a labor detail—could manually enter data into the sensor pods.

Other than the panel's second co-chairman, Sen. Bob Smith, not a single committee member attended this public hearing. But McCain, having been advised of Alfond's testimony, suddenly rushed into the room to confront her. His face angry and his voice very loud, he accused her of making allegations . . . that were totally false and deceptive."

Making a fist, he shook his index finger at her and said she had insulted an emissary to Vietnam sent by President Bush. He said she had insulted other MIA families with her remarks.

And then he said, through clenched teeth: "And I am sick and tired of you insulting mine and other people's [patriotism] who happen to have different views than yours."

## BROUGHT TO TEARS

By this time, tears were running down Alfond's cheeks. She reached into her handbag for a handkerchief. She tried to speak: "The family members have been waiting for years—years! And now you're shutting down." He kept interrupting her. She tried to say, through tears, that she had issued no insults. He kept talking over her words. He said she was accusing him and others of "some conspiracy without proof, and some cover-up."

She said she was merely seeking "some answers. That is what I am asking." He ripped into her for using the word "fiasco." She replied: "The fiasco was the people that stepped out and said we have written the end, the final chapter to Vietnam." "No one said that," he shouted. "No one said what you are saying they said, Ms. Alfond." And then, his face flaming pink, he stalked out of the room, to shouts of disfavor from members of the audience.

As with most of McCain's remarks to Alfond, the facts in his closing blast at her were incorrect. Less than three weeks earlier, on Oct. 23, 1992, in a ceremony in the White House Rose Garden, President Bush—with John McCain standing beside him—said: "Today, finally, I am convinced that we can begin writing the last chapter in the Vietnam War."

## PENNSYLVANIA LEGISLATURE

Dolores Alfond also testified, before the Pennsylvania Legislature, May 3, 1999, on behalf of American servicemen left behind at the end of the Korean War. She commended the members of the legislature for the introduction of Senate Resolution No. 25 "Memorializing the President and the Congress to take whatever action is necessary to obtain the release of Americans being held against their will in North Korea." She commented that in 1953, at the conclusion of the Korean War, the families of those who had not returned realized something was very wrong, that North Korea had not returned all of our Prisoners of War. And a year later the POW families had begun hearing that many of our POWs had been transferred to China and the former Soviet Union. What shocked the families is that the U.S. government "dismissed these family members as distraught wives, mothers, fathers, brothers, sisters and children who could not accept their loved ones' deaths." To fight back, the Korean War POW/MIA families united to form the Fighting Home Folks, an organization that although no longer in existence began the decades-long struggle to discover the truth about POW/MIAs. The Fighting Home Folks spoke of Chinese involvement in the movement of U.S. POWs from Korea, of American prisoners of war in Siberia, and the U.S. government denied it all. Of all of this, Ms. Alfond commented: "Officials dismissed the Vietnam families and their information. . . . Today, we know just how accurate 'The Fighting Home Folks' and their information [were]."

Finally, on March 26th, 1996, I.O. Lee of the Defense POW/MIA Office prepared a memo titled "Accountability of Missing Americans From the Korean War—Live Sighting Reports," admitting that the government had received numerous reports concerning Americans living or detained in North Korea after the prisoner exchanges with North Korea in 1953. The report concluded that there were live American sightings in North Korea, a small group of defectors and a larger group of 10 - 15 possible POWs. The report concluded: "there are too many live sighting reports, specifically observations of several Caucasians in a collective farm . . . (to say that) there are no American POWs in North Korea." Two Romanian citizens working in a North Korean factory in Pyongyang were on a North Korean government sponsored sightseeing trip. Both of them testified that the Caucasian farmers they saw along the roadside were American prisoners of war. Ms. Alfond also quotes Col. Philip Corso's 1996 testimony during congressional hearings: "In the past I have tried to tell Congress the fact that in 1953, 500 sick and wounded American prisoners were within 10 miles of a collection point."

She also quotes a Foreign Service Information Broadcast (FBIS) Report, dated December 12, 1996, that stated: "A man claiming to be a North Korean defector said he once lived with

American and South Korean prisoners of war whose names were formally verified as missing in action (MIA) from the 1950 - 1953 Korean War." At this point in our narrative we have ceased being shocked at the manner in which our government handled the POW/MIA Issue, but another reference by Ms. Alfond brings us back to reality. A 44-page "air intelligence information report," dated 19 October 1955 described existing evidence of live American POWs not repatriated during Operation Big Switch and Operation Little Switch, men who were in Kasson awaiting repatriation, men known "to be alive in Communist hands as of the close of the Korean conflict, July '53." A Kim Yong-Hwa, who came to Seoul via China, said he met an American named "John Smith" during a training session in May 1971 at Taechon Airfield in north Pyongan Province. Smith had been captured with another colleague while fighting at Changjin, South Hamgyong province in North Korea. Ms Alfond cited other cases.

## THE FOUR BILLION DOLLAR OFFER

Alfond continued to discuss an offer made by the North Koreans in the fall of 1997 to negotiate for "American survivors" held in North Korea. The White House turned down the offer, making the hasty judgment that the offer was just an empty gesture, but it was not. Ms. Alfond knows that the offer was not an empty gesture because in the spring of 1997 she personally met with representatives of the DPRK (North Korea) in New York City as a prelude to the unprecedented offer, by the North Koreans, to negotiate for American survivors. It all collapsed when the White House refused to cooperate in the negotiations. As Ms Alfond remarked: "There is no explanation as to why the Clinton administration termed the offer for American 'survivors' an 'empty gesture.' We would think that any information relating to this nation's 'highest national priority' would be acted on immediately." To make matters worse, she reports that in order to take the story of living servicemen in North Korea, the Pentagon blitzed the press with the story of an excavation site and the announcement that the Pentagon was sending a delegation to North Korea to witness an excavation and possible remains recovery. As widely reported, the Pentagon pressured North Korea to extend an invitation to a family member to visit a site currently being excavated. The story "successfully diverted the attention from 'live men' to "remains" . . . . By sending this new delegation to North Korea, they gave the media a new focus and American 'survivors' were quickly forgotten."

What were we coming to when the enemy wants to talk about returning our POWs and the U.S. government rejects the offer? Time has passed and all the men involved in this tawdry matter may have passed away before time catches up with them, but one day they may all be "tried and sentenced" *in memoriam*. Ms Alfond reminded the senators that the POWs alive today in North Korea, China and the former Soviet Union have waited long enough and their families have waited long enough, and yet our live POWs "do not factor into any of our negotiations with North Korea. Instead of asking for live men, we ask for remains and access to archives." The incredible and inexplicable actions of our government over the last 50 years continue unabated. As Ms. Alfond poignantly asked the senators, "How much longer must our POWs wait?"

**LT. COL. BO GRITZ**

# CHAPTER NINE

# THE REMARKABLE BO GRITZ

**James "Bo" Gritz on November 23, 1992** testified before the Senate select committee. Gritz outlined his involvement in POW/MIA matters in a 22-page deposition. He states very clearly his opinion that over the preceding 12 years that officials within the Executive Branch of the U.S. government (USG) knowingly abandoned U.S. prisoners of war (POWs) held by Communists during and after World War I, World War II, Korea and Southeast Asia (the Vietnam War), and the present Bush administration knows that Americans were left alive and in violation of law have continued and perpetrated a cover up. He believes that certain members of the U.S. Congress aided in the diversion of vital information that could have given the American people all the information we needed to find and rescue our POWs. Ashamed of this, and not wanting the truth of their incompetence and private political and economic agendas to become known, many in the American government find that the only way to protect themselves is to discredit the living POW movement and those who support it. As Gritz pointed out: "It may not be economically or politically expedient for the USG to deal with the POW Issue . . . it is my view that for U.S. officials to look interested posing with Communist officials before stacks of old uniforms and equipment is an insult to the heroes who once were a part of it." The fact is that the Laotian Communists did not return our POWs, the Vietnamese withheld POWs after 1973, and Americans who were sent to Russia were never returned."

Bo told it like it is, and we should tell it like it is come the 2008 elections. Let us not ask the politicians in our district what it is we can do to make them richer. Let us ask them what they will do for our POWs if we reelect them. And if we are not satisfied with their answers, let us throw them out. We want more information rather than boots, helmets, pistols et al. As Gritz insists, we want our boys back.

## OPERATION LIBERATOR

Deputy Director of the Defense Intelligence Agency (DIA), Lt. Gen. Harold R. Aaron, said: "I asked Bo in October 1978 to go in search of U.S. prisoners of war in Southeast Asia. At that time, he was assigned to the U.S. Army Element, Office of the Secretary of Defense as a chief of congressional relations. At the same time, Gen. Tighe, director, DIA, asked Ross Perot to sponsor a private effort to find our guys, and Perot called Bo, inviting him to his Dallas office in April 1979 and made a request. Gritz described the scene:

"[Perot said:] 'I want you to go over there and see everyone you have to see, do all the things you need to do. [If ] you come back and tell me there aren't any American prisoners left alive, I [won't] believe it. And I'm not interested in bones.'

"Col. Arthur D. 'Bull' Simons was there. . . . He told me: 'I'm going to plan the operation, and you're going to execute it.' I left for Asia immediately. Bull Simons died while I was away."

Gritz left for Southeast Asia to prove that all our POWs were not home. He returned convinced that some of our POWs were still alive. A Vietnamese named Nguyen Giang was in a refugee camp, having escaped from Vietnam. He said he was with 49 American POWs only months before. Two of the POWs had died, and Giang buried them. The others were still alive at the time of his escape. The Americans were being held at Tan Lop, a camp near the Red River, north of Hanoi. Gritz reported this to Perot and recommended that Giang be made available for interrogation, by electronic and chemical means, for verification of his claim. Perot contacted Gen. Tighe and requested that Giang be brought to the States; Tighe passed on the request to Secretary of Defense Harold Brown, who then forwarded the recommendation to Secretary of State Cyrus Vance. A month later, Vance declined.

Gritz points out that although the executive branch denied

this exchange of letters, he had copies in his possession. Now, what in the name of heaven would possess a secretary of state to deny access to a man identified as having seen American POWs and who can say exactly where they are? What reason of state was more important than the return of 47 abandoned American prisoners of war? We have a right to know what it was! We the American people have a right to make judgments on an official who would commit such a heinous act as to deny this nation access to a man whom our own investigators assert can give us exact information about the fact and the whereabouts of American prisoners of war. We still have that right. The fact that Vance got away with it then does not preclude his being investigated and questioned now about the basis for his refusal to get the facts.

Gritz told the committee that he returned to Southeast Asia to continue the search. "Patrols were launched into Laos to suspected POW holding areas using forces loyal to Gen. Vang Pao [CIA mercenary chief, Military Region II—Laos, during the war]." One unit returned with a sighting of 30 U.S. POWs at Nhommarath, Laos, and satellite photography confirmed "30 non-Asians by measurable shadow" and a figure 52 made in the ground, visible by air. The Nhommarath report became "top secret - special intelligence"! (This is another example of the misuse of the classification of documents. Documents are to be classified only to keep information from an enemy.) Once again, Adm. Tuttle told Gritz that he briefed President-elect Reagan on the finding in the West Wing of the White House in January 1981. The information was so sensitive that Gritz was told by Tuttle "never to even say the word Nhommarath"!

## OPERATION VELVET HAMMER

Gritz then formed a pilot team in Florida to begin initial planning for a possible private sector rescue effort, but Gritz was told by Adm. Tuttle in his Pentagon office to stand down: "President Reagan is excited and intends to make the rescue using Delta Force." Gritz was afraid that politics would intervene, just as it did in the Bay of Pigs invasion, with President Kennedy withholding air support at the last minute. However, Tuttle assured him that that would not happen. The team he had assembled was dispersed after Bo learned that a Delta force was being assembled for the rescue in Ft. Bragg. Nevertheless he was nagged by the thought that, in the end, Reagan's staff would not be willing to take the risk of sending an official military force into Laos because the helicopter-borne force would have to enter a high-risk corridor across Vietnam.

Such was his anxiety that Bo wrote a top-secret memo to President Reagan outlining his own alternative. The message was delivered to National Security Advisor Richard Allen on 30 March 1981, the day Reagan was shot. Bo was told that Haig disapproved of his plan. Tuttle advised him to be alert for a witch-hunt, and informed him that he was recommending to Lt. Gen. Phillip Gast, JCS Operations chief, that he be brought back on active duty to head up the operation. On May 20th Tuttle called him at his Los Angeles home bringing the bad news that the next day's *Washington Post* would carry a front-page story stating that CIA mercenaries were sent into Laos looking for POWs, but found none. The operation had been cancelled. Another disappointment. Another lie had been fed to the American people via *The Washington Post* on an issue so important to the American soul and psyche.

## OPERATION LAZARUS

Gritz launched Operation Lazarus with the help of Fred O'Green, CEO of Litton Industries, who supplied him with night vision and fire control communication devices, even though the mission did not have Adm. Paulson's blessing. Bo Gritz spent the summer and fall of 1982 setting up the operation within Thailand. Gordon Wilson informed President Reagan in the Santa Barbara White House. Gritz made two incursions into Laos in November and December 1982. A guerrilla organization was trained in the use of HF radios, codes, cameras and special reconnaissance techniques. Laotian Gen. Kham Bou Phimasen surveyed the target sites. On 10 January 1983, Gritz was told that one of the targets contained live U.S. POWs. At that point O'Green said that operational funds had been cut off and no return was authorized. However, after some negotiating Gritz was given permission to return. He, Scott Weekly and Gary Goldman re-entered Laos 30 January 1983 and spent the next 30 days in an attempt to rescue POWs. Then, inexplicably, Gritz received messages from the CIA instructing him to return at once.

A State Department representative named Mulkey visited them but was not authorized to discuss any conversations related to the POW Issue. ASA (Army Security Agency) personnel told them that their instructions were to find the group and keep an eye on them. It appeared to Gritz that one arm of the government was authorizing operations but that as soon as they got under way, another arm, presumably at a higher level, called them off. In Gritz's words, "DOD's demeaning treatment of our good-faith effort was to become standard fare from a bureaucracy determined to keep its skeletons hidden! For some reason it was 'kill the messenger' instead of 'seek the truth.'"

Gritz was frustrated. "Adm. Jerry O. Tuttle told me that he personally briefed the president! It was A-1 top secret special intelligence. He was a key DIA-POW official."

An effort was coordinated to bring three Americans to the Thai side of the Mekong River near Si Chiang Mai, west of Vientiane, Laos during the Christmas-New Year period 1984-85. A Laotian police colonel was assigned the task of taking Broken Wing [code name for the operatives] in his truck from the camp to rendezvous with the others at the river. The son and six defecting Pathet Lao guards were to escort the other two Americans on foot. One of the three POWs was described as having the use of only one leg.

Gritz was asked to testify before a Solarz subcommittee hearing in March 1983. He was asked if he had any government sponsorship of his search for POWs and he responded that he had but that he could not reveal from what agency in open session. During that period of time, the *Washington Post* revealed, "Reagan was told to rein in rogue intelligence operations." All of Gritz's

work and that of the men who worked with him was characterized as unauthorized and without value. His government abandoned and discredited him. He was defamed and lied about by
U.S. government officials. This was and remains, absolutely dis-
graceful, and perfidy at its worst.

## THE CASE OF WALTER HUGH MOON

Insults did not prevent Gritz from proceeding in his POW
quest. He and Gary Goldman traveled to Paris to consult with
Chinese Gen. Kong Le, who was told that a son of one of his former officers was in charge of three U.S. POWs at a camp near
Xieng Khouang, Laos. Bo contacted the father along the Thai border northeast of Vientiane.

At the appointed time and place a reconnaissance/boat team
was sent across the river to pick up those who had arrived. Contact was made and the party started back in two dug-out boats
(pirogues). Mid-stream the lead boat was taken under fire by a
patrol boat hidden alongside an island. The boat then ran down
what was left. The second pirogue was seen to turn back and
successfully make land. Agents reported the two Americans safe.
Two dead and two wounded members of the Gritz team were recovered by the Thais. The Gritz team tried throughout the week
to arrange another pick-up, without success. Then Gritz's reconnaissance team made contact with the POWs and their guards
by radio. As they were about to launch a rubber boat to pick up
the POWs, gunfire erupted. The attempt failed.

Evidence of the sighting and proof of access to the POWs
came in the form of producing Lance Peter Sijan's U.S. Air Force
Academy ring for a reward of $1,000 and a photo-signature of
MIA Special Forces Maj. Walter H. Moon, who was missing in action April 22, 1961. The ring contained the proper Balfour markings, class date '65, wear marks, and inside the inscribed name
of "Lance Peter Sijan." The photo produced by the source was a
full-face close-up of a bearded Caucasian in prison garb with a
bandaged head. A scrap of paper contained three written notes:
The name, Walter Hugh Moon, the date of birth, 31 March 1923,

and the place of birth, Rudy, Arkansas, USA. The note was signed "Walter H. Moon." Gritz claims he was told that Assistant Secretary of Defense Richard Armitage considered the ring a fake. Gritz observed, "I was puzzled at the refusal and angry that a high government official like Armitage would be so quick to powerfully discredit something without so much as an examination or inquiry. Armitage's knee-jerk reaction was standard Pentagon response to any private sector offering." Gritz handed the photo, negative and "signature of prisoner" to Chairman Solarz of the House POW subcommittee and to the DIA. Gritz asks, "Why wasn't the Moon document ever presented to the Laotian authorities for explanation and possible resolution?" Character assassination was just one of the many tools government officials, senators and congressmen used to cover up both their lack of dedication to the POW Issue and their lack of expertise.

## OPERATION SOUTHSIDE

Gritz continued his desire to locate the three MIA POWs and someone helped him to meet a man who claimed to represent a Pathet Lao general officer who wanted to make a deal with the United States. The general would be willing to turn over five U.S. POWs in exchange for safe passage for his family. The source said the general would personally escort the senior U.S. prisoner to a point near the border, where Gritz would meet them. It was assumed to be Richard A. Walsh, who was shot down flying an A-1J Skyraider on 15 February 1969. Gritz questioned the wisdom of a general officer driving a U.S. POW along Route 23 and 9 through roadblocks assumed to be occupied by Vietnamese. Gritz was told the general had authority and passes to allow such a trip and that he should only be concerned with safely negotiating the border to arrive at a point just north of Savannakhet. Once Walsh was safe, Gritz was to arrange acceptance of family belonging to the general and several of his key officers. Four more Americans were to accompany them across the border into Thailand. In the planning, Gritz gave the go-between a U.S. passport to be used as ID by Walsh once the exchange took place. The passport was necessary to guarantee that the Thais would not arrest Walsh if he were to be spotted as required once we crossed into Thailand and before he was returned to U.S. control. The Thais supported our efforts throughout.

Christmas-New Year 1985-86 was the target date. But all did not go as planned. Gritz received a report that both the general and his passenger had been intercepted and were being detained by the enemy. A report in the press stated that the Laotians and Vietnamese claimed that they had "apprehended and were holding a U.S. citizen" provided the only evidence. However, shortly after returning to the United States, Gritz chatted with a friend, Col. Nestor Pino, at the State Department, who said, "Good to see you alive. We thought maybe you had been captured—your passport turned up in a strange place." This caused Gritz to wonder why U.S. officials did not act on the report of an American in custody.

## OPERATION EMERALD CITY

Harvey called Gritz in late October 1986 from the White House (NSC) with the news that Vice President Bush was aware of the detention of POWS by a drug lord in Burma. Bush's report said that "Khun Sa" [a pseudonym meaning "Prince Prosperous"] had five POWs and sightings on 70 more, and that Khun Sa had lost four of the POWs by drowning while attempting to cross the Mekong River. The DIA, CIA and DEA had not verified the VP's report, "but it came from very highly placed and reliable sources." Harvey asked Gritz if he were able to confirm the report and added that President Reagan was prepared to do whatever was required to get the men back. To accomplish this it would be vital to receive the cooperation of Gen. Khun Sa. Gritz and Scott Weekly flew to Washington to meet Harvey, and he handed them a letterhead and language that identified them to Khun Sa. Subsequently, they left for Burma. To assist them they formed a Malaysian- Mandarin Chinese ethnic agent unit, since Khun Sa spoke Mandarin. This enabled them to gain entry inside Khun Sa's headquarters, only to discover that the reports of his having American POWs were not true. Gritz wanted to be able to verify Khun Sa's statement that he had no POWs so he videoed Khun Sa's statement and even asked him to take a polygraph test. Although Khun Sa could not offer any evidence of the whereabouts of the POWs he did offer to send agents to look for them in Laos along a north-south line running from Vientiane as far as the Burma border. He promised to either care for any Americans found and hand them over to U.S. authorities or entrust Gritz with 2,500 of his best troops to look for them. Gritz was told to return in March for the results.

Their discussion also included the question of the traffic in heroin. Khun Sa was willing to dismantle all Golden Triangle opiate operations and even to provide a list of his best customers of the previous 20 years. In return, the U.S. would sign a trade agreement which would guarantee the development of the Shan State's natural resources. It was an offer the U.S. could not refuse, but it did. In December 1986 Harvey notified Gritz that the U.S. would not go along with the trade agreement, and Gritz's reaction to that was, "Such a negative response was surprising, but staff assistants in D.C. tend to develop tunnel vision and see no importance outside of their own narrow focus. I returned to Burma and found reason why there was 'no interest'!"

In April of 1986, Gritz returned to Burma because of newspaper reports that "Khun Sa's mountain stronghold had been seized," and the newspapers reported that the "U.S. Declares No Mercy in Drug War Against Khun Sa." It was also reported that a task force of 26,000 soldiers had dismantled the Shan State and removed Khun Sa. That appeared very strange indeed since Khun Sa continued to send messages to Gritz inviting him back, so he determined to return and find out what was going on. Upon my arrival I discovered that there was no battle going on, no war on Khun Sa at all, and, in fact, the border was wide open. Together with Lance Trimmer and Barry Flynn as observers, Gritz arrived comfortably at Khun Sa's headquarters by truck, instead of by horse as he had previously been forced to do.

Khun Sa was alive and well, sporting a new crew-cab Toyota, along with a new hospital and a beautiful new temple. There had been, in spite of newspaper reports to the contrary, no war, no attack on Khun Sa's opium empire. As he greeted Gritz he laughed and asked him what took him so long. Gritz was embarrassed to tell him that he had been waiting for the reported but non-existent war to die down. It had all been a hoax, and the U.S. government was complicit in it. That was the reason why the State Department was not interested in Khun Sa's offer of a trade agreement.

Khun Sa explained: "After you left with my Reagan message in December, I thought maybe I'd see B-52 bombers overhead. Instead both the Thais and Burmese came to me and said they had to make it look like they were doing something or they could lose millions of U.S. drug suppression dollars. I told them to do anything they wanted as long as it included a road from Mae Hong Son Airport."

Ten-ton trucks had replaced the horses and mules as the increase in drug tonnage quickly indicated. A news article showing the U.S. ambassador presenting the Thais with a $1.8 million check for all their hard work was very likely the butt of jokes throughout Asia. Khun Sa, however, said that although his agents had turned up no evidence of U.S. prisoners alive in western Laos, he was willing to reveal some of the U.S. officials he had dealt with since winning the Burma-Laos Opium War in 1967. Gritz was stunned to hear that Richard Armitage was the person who handled the money with the banks in Australia. Gritz was familiar with the Nugan-Hand Bank chain that laundered CIA drug money worldwide and points out that the Chiang Mai branch telephone was answered by the DEA secretary. Mike Hand had been a Special Forces operative. Nugan was found shot to death after word of the bank's dealings was revealed, and Hand disappeared.

Gritz concludes that if Armitage was indeed the bagman, then he wouldn't want live POWs coming home. Follow-on investigations would involve him as the responsible bureaucrat. Armitage and Harvey lifted weights together at the Pentagon Officers Athletic Club: "If Armitage was involved and saw Khun Sa's offer to name names, it could have sparked the 'newspaper drug war'—

something certainly did!" Armitage later became the Assistant Secretary of State under Colin Powell during the first Administration of George Bush.

## OPERATION RED BULL

Gritz left again for Thailand in January 1987 to follow-up on POW leads from various sources. Upon arriving in Bangkok, he was offered a room in the prime minister's quadrangle. Som Suk [an agent for the Red Bull union, similar to America's Teamsters] was preparing to travel to Vientiane, Laos with the Minister of Commerce to speak with Kaysone Phomvihan [Prime Minister of Laos] about an upcoming rice deal. Gritz quotes Som Suk as saying that he had spoken with Kaysone in social conversation about the possibility of buying out U.S. POWs. Kaysone told him that there were two Americans near death being held in Vientiane and two more not far away. The entire operation could be kept secret, he said, and the Americans could be officially listed as having died in captivity when they were actually being secretly transferred to U.S. control. The prime minister asked, "How much do you think we could get?" When Som Suk replied, "10 million bahts for each," Kaysone's response was, "Good; that's 8 million for me and 2 million for you."

Som Suk asked Gritz if he had acted properly in making the offer of 10 million bahts, and Gritz assured him that that was fine. Then followed a meeting to set up the transfer of the POWs with lawyers and persons representing Kaysone. A Thai special forces general would provide security from Udorn to Ban. Gritz was to carry a bank voucher showing sufficient funds in an "overseas account" for the transaction.

Once the money was in-country, the Laotians would produce positive ID of four U.S. POWs, and the first deposit of 10 million bahts would be made into the "in-country account" followed by the handing over of the first live American.

Subsequent transfers would occur in the same manner. But the money never arrived, and the angry Laotians returned home, as did a bitterly disappointed Som Suk. Gritz speculates that: "It is conceivable that Harvey relayed the information to Assistant Secretary of Defense Richard Armitage, who was responsible for POW/MIA recovery and 'other arrangements' were made that cut me out of the net."

## THREATS FROM U.S. OFFICIALS

As soon as Gritz returned to a Bangkok safe house on 19 May 1987, he received a call from Joseph Felter, who informed him that U.S. government authorities wished to pass on the message that Gritz should "erase and forget everything I had just learned from Khun Sa and return IMMEDIATELY with all documentation to be turned over to Harvey upon arrival. My failure to properly respond would 'hurt the U.S. government.'" Felter called Gritz a second time on 29 May in LA at the request of William Davis, a State Department official, to "warn me about any disclosure of Khun Sa information. I was told that if I did not cooperate, aggravated charges and hostile witnesses would be brought against me—that I would serve 15 years as a felon. My oath was not to lie, shred or cover up. I chose instead to present the information and was called to testify before Larry Smith's House Subcommittee on Narcotics Oversight. It was a mistake. Smith did not allow the members to view the Khun Sa video record. . . . He said the charges against Armitage were old, investigated and unfounded."

The DEA finally admitted to a new road from Mae Hong Son to Khun Sa's HQ, but called it a "graduation road." Khun Sa wanted Thai officials to attend a special ceremony and didn't want them riding mules for miles. Official heroin statistics record that in 1986 Khun Sa shipped 600 tons of opiates out of his Golden Triangle. The amount went up to 900 in 1987 (per highway), then 1,200 tons in 1988 and 3,050 tons in 1989. Attorney General Richard Thornburgh indicted Khun Sa, calling him the world's blackest criminal. Khun Sa offered President George Bush one metric ton of #4 pure Asian heroin that sells for over $1 million per pound on the street in major American cities. It was to be a show of good faith.

Then Bo started to feel the heat. He was charged in Oklahoma

City for training Afghans, and in Los Angeles for violation of the Neutrality Act. The FBI came to his rescue, and the charges were dropped. Then he was indicted in Las Vegas for using a false passport. When, after two years the government could not stop him from talking about government drug operations and POWs, he was taken before a sealed Classified Information Procedures Act (CIPA) hearing. White House, NSC, State Department, and Justice Department officials testified. Judge Phillip Pro ruled the only thing Bo could talk about before the jury was that a high-level U.S. intelligence agency official asked him to go in pursuit of U.S. POWs. "I was acquitted, but had been prevented from travel for two years. On May 9th, 1989, State Department Special Agent Scott Farquar made an official statement: "Let me start by telling you that Gritz has been confirmed to have been an agent of the Intelligence Support Activity (ISA) of the United States Army. His mission and the mission of the ISA are deemed to be classified."

Well done, Bo Gritz. The nation will always be grateful to you for working honestly and diligently while being supervised by some who were dishonest and unfeeling, men and women who had agendas not known about and not shared by the American people.

'On your knees!'

# CHAPTER TEN

# MAJOR MARK SMITH SPEAKS OUT

MAJ. MARK SMITH SUBMITTED HIS THOUGHTS TO THE AUTHORS in the summer of 2007:

To most people the case for POWS being left behind only appears as a snapshot versus the terrible Technicolor tragedy it truly is. People who have seen the snapshots of evidence eventually explained away, sometimes in the most bizarre of ways, ask "Why?" after losing focus and hope. You see, if you are of good conscience, you must kill off the POWs before you move on in your life. Thus at some point of age, health, crisis or just boredom, too many resign themselves to the convenient "put it out of our mind" route traveled by the U.S. government since World War II. Our government's answer to those who were left in the hands of an implacable enemy was to abandon them with the stroke of a pen. Those who just wish to get on with their lives must do the same. They, in some way, become as helpful to our POWs as the enemies they opposed.

America has a fairly short history of amazing accomplishments compared to the rest of the world. We are the "quick fix" guys. We are not great at the long haul. Thus, our leaders have cajoled us with less than truthful accounts of the "heroic deaths" of our missing men (and women).

That there has been, over the decades, little or no proof of their actual demise, has caused us to invent a complete story out of what we do not know or have reluctantly chosen to deny as truth. This is why the only American to return after the war was given a punishment that equally guilty POWs, who returned in 1973, never received. Other blatant collaborators were literally sent home after asking to stay in Communist Vietnam. Why would they "allow to stay" the least well-trained in the group of those applying, a Marine private first class? The true answer is that they didn't "allow him to stay"; they kept him, and too many others.

Many consider Garwood the most unlucky participant in the Vietnam War, but he is not. Bob Garwood is the luckiest man on planet Earth. He got himself out of Vietnam in the same time frame President James Earl Carter killed all [POWs] except one, with the stroke of a pen. You see, the U.S. government has a convenient answer for any who should appear after the pen has killed them; "Those who want to be there." No member of the "mainstream" media has ever asked a U.S. official how dead people could "want" to be anywhere.

What drives people like Holland and me? Actually, it is the never-ending evidence so amateurishly explained away and accepted by the media that drives us. Initials and numbers attributed before the war's end to a specific missing American, somehow morph into a "natural occurrence" when he does not return from prison. This means he died in the crash of his aircraft. The team sent into the crash area found bloody bandages and fully deployed parachutes, not belonging to the two known survivors who were rescued. The U.S. government will tell you their "experts" determined the fire in the aircraft had burnt through the pack trays of the chutes and they deployed on their own with no one in the harness. If pushed they would probably show you a standard Army T-10 parachute with the cloth breakaway cord holding the parachute in the tray until the static-line breaks it and deploys the chute.

But these were Air Force emergency rigs with heavy nylon covers and held in place by stainless steel pins and grommets. Every expert I talked to says the nylon and silk would fuse in a fire ball before the heat could melt through the steel and nylon protecting the chute. The piles of bloody bandages found in the area of the deployed para-chutes are attributed to wounded enemy person-nel. The report of the action when the CAS team went in mentions no such heavy fighting or a time when enemy troops wounded in the action could have produced the piles of bloody bandages or dressed their wounds and walked away leaving their bandages on the ground. Thankfully the true myth spinners of the POW/MIA Issue make no attempt to explain why a wounded man would take this stupid action.

The wife of the individual who the initials were attributed to and who was a table navigator on this flight, journeyed to the crash-site in the early seventies. There was not much there, but she found a small shard of bone. This she duti-fully turned in to the USG upon her return, and her name was put on it as the person turning it in. Fast-forward many years and the U.S. govern-ment, along with the ever-"helpful" Laotians, ex-cavated the crash site. They were able to come up with a few more shards of bone, and Capt.

Thomas T. Hart was now ready to be buried. The government demanded to do this even though forensic anthropologists stated that no determination could be made as to whom these few shards of bone belonged to or if they were even Caucasian. But when his wife Ann, the mother of six children, looked at the "remains" there was the bone she herself had turned in from the early seventies. She, being a very smart lady, had some real questions on the laws of probability: For instance, the chances a lady from Live Oak, Florida could travel thousands of miles, walk into a virtually barren field and find, out of a dozen people missing, a tiny piece of bone belonging to her own husband.

Do not tell me who makes up stories about MIAs. Because then I must tell you of my agent in the early 1980s who brought for repair in Thailand, a partial plate he claimed belonged to Capt. Hart, containing the same number of teeth he had lost playing football in Live Oak, Florida. A mistake or misunderstanding? No, it was a crime against an honorable warrior and his family. I wish with all my heart I could tell you the above is an isolated case, but it is not. It is shameful the way proficient and honorable men are made to look foolish. Maj. Albro Lundy, an instructor pilot, forgot to attach his leg straps on his parachute and fell out of it and surely died. According to his government, the man who trained others to "do it by the numbers" was not capable of doing that himself. That, sir, is not an explanation; it is an insult. Later they claimed to have found the same man's remains at the place his aircraft crashed. One can but wonder what a physics major would make of the probability of a man punching out of his aircraft, falling out of his parachute and then by some unknown force being propelled to link up with his aircraft and crash with it. I would not bet on this probability if Einstein rigged it himself, but my government did.

Sometimes it is better to say you just do not know than to make up these stories as you go along. This does no service to a man who may well be dead. My government makes much of someone like Private Garwood being a "coward" and "collaborator." But they also go to great lengths to create the "heroic death." I give you the case of my own subordinate SFC Howard Lull, who according to the U.S. government "went down fighting" at a bridge south of Loc Ninh, South Vietnam, on 8 April 1972. He was awarded the Silver Star, our nation's third highest award for gallantry in action.

SFC Lull was with me on the evening of 7 April 1972 as I led him and a handful of Vietnamese in an attempt to escape and evade capture. I had been wounded numerous times, but Lull had only superficial shrapnel wounds. As we crossed the road south of the camp, through the bombing going on, we were ambushed by a squad of NVA and we shot it out with them. I was hit through my bowel; it filled with blood, and I pulled down my pants to empty it. As I squatted in this position my sergeant looked at me and said: "You aren't going to make it, and one of us has to get out and tell what you did here."

I cried. He and most of the Vietnamese just turned around and walked away. The next morning a Vietnamese doctor and I were captured in a shootout and my Cambodian bodyguard, Corp. Hen, was murdered when he spat on the NVA. He was the ONLY doctor who left the camp with SFC Lull and me. NVA Lt. Gen. Tran Van Tra, whose headquarters I was captured in, invited me to breakfast. I asked about any other captives and he said: "We have SFC Lull, but he does not want to go with you." Intelligence points to Lull surviving and prospering to this day in Vietnam.

What does the U.S. government say happened to SFC Lull? DIA says that Lull died heroically fighting at the Cam Very Bridge south of Loc Ninh. Who was their witness to this heroism? He was the very same doctor who was captured with me and was released with me. The only thing the doctor saw Lull do was to desert. So who are really those who make up stories about POW/MIAs? It is, in fact, many of those who said that innocent and courageous sources made up stories. And many of these folks sat in the White House and in the halls of Congress. The evidence is compelling, but if you want to test it in court both the executive and legislative branches of government will fight you tooth and nail. Both branches have been accustomed to trying every nasty tactic to obtain everything you possess without having a judge see it. The reason seems to be that both have failed our POWs on numerous occasions only to use them for convenient "face-time" in front of the media, and then kill them again with the stroke of a pen. A case in point is Sen. John Kerry, who came to Bangkok, Thailand and threatened me with a legal summons to appear before him and Sen. John McCain's Senate committee. I said there was no need for that and I would make myself available. I was never called. McCain says it was because I had once invited six-foot-six-inch Sen. Alan Simpson out to the parking lot to box after he called me less than honorable and described evidence I provided the committee as "lightweight stuff."

Surely all these tall, good looking senators are not afraid of one five-foot-eight-and-one-half-inch retired infantry major? No, they are not; but they are scared to death about what one might say about their carefully crafted lie that they "know" all POWs came home in 1973.

My country has done a great disservice against my fellow Americans missing and captured. The stories they make up run from a Navy Corpsman on a recon deep in enemy territory, "deserting" in the heat of battle, to somehow join a girlfriend, to turning an AWOL Marine into a POW camp escape artist who died heroically. One would think they could be caring and competent enough to at least point the accusing finger at the right people, especially since there are numerous witnesses stating neither is dead. The Communists would threaten me with never going home: "We have a place, and if you are sent there, you will never go home." I believe that statement is one of the few true things they ever said during my captivity. I fully believe they sent too many of my brethren to that place.

I would like to recount a meeting with a brave enemy commander. I know he was brave and competent because he captured me. He invited me back to meet with him before he died. He knew well of my efforts to bring home POWs from Southeast Asia. He smiled at me and said: "Still the hardhead." He then told me how, as the NVA representative to the four-party peace agreement staff, he had asked for a helicopter in 1973 to pick up a group of unreleased POWs in the delta of South Vietnam. Instead of simply providing the helicopter his American counterpart felt he should go to Hanoi and ask permission. The NVA general was removed by his government, and the release did not take place. The NVA general's name was Tran Van Tra.

## THE REACHING OUT TO REFUGEES MYTH

Some refugees had made a fairly decent life for themselves once re-education was completed. But they were plagued with a nagging sense of loyalty to an ally and a group of fellow soldiers they had served beside in war. Many had heard, seen and in some cases actually been held with American POWS kept by the communists long after the war. One constant in their minds was their belief the U.S. government would want to know. This proved to be a totally misplaced trust in a former ally. Soon word began to filter back into Vietnam, Laos and Cambodia; "DO NOT MENTION POWS."

By prior agreement, we would go to the Lao/Cambodian/ Vietnamese governments and ask to speak to a particular individual. Then the government, which would be guilty of an international war-crime if the data is true, contacts their citizen and sets up a meeting with the U.S. side, weeks or months down the road. The original source then denies to the U.S. team that he ever claimed knowledge of U.S. POWs. Just another "scam" or "misunderstanding" ironed out by those best of friends, the U.S. government and the Lao/Cambodian/VN Communists? No, in my book our government has just assisted a bellicose regime in identifying and beating down another voice of dissent and possible source of critical intelligence. I can personally attest to the fact that though this looks so benign on paper, it is brutal in its application by the Communist governments in question. Are we merely playing at the search for POWS or are we truly this stupid or, worse, this cruel? I fear it is the latter. Why has the U.S. government never released easily obtainable overhead imagery of the area in northern Vietnam where the much-discussed "dairy farm" is located? After all, this place has been discussed going back to the Vietnam War when it was believed French POWS were still being held there along with Americans. Did anyone come home in 1973 from this well-known location?

NO! If the so-called "Fort Apache" photos did not contain individuals who, when their shadows were measured appeared to be westerners, why has the U.S. government never released the photos to prove its point? How is it that the U.S. government never points out that there is no use of the Roman alphabet in the areas of Laos where they try to discredit Roman letters appearing on the ground in overhead imagery? The U.S. position is that the locals might have done it. In other words, our government wants us to believe that it is not American downed pilots who did this, but locals who do not have a clue about and have never used the Roman alphabet. They just decide to cut, burn or stamp, T TH, SEREX or U.S.A. into the ground for laughs? The story of a villager receiving an airmail letter from a relative in the U.S.A. and going out to cut it into the landscape because he liked the design is hogwash. If government "servants" are going to lie, at the very least they should come up with something plausible. In some cases a refugee reports seeing a certain American and gives at least a variation of his name. Why do we not give him more credibility if he says the man is "Black," if the missing man with that name is in fact "Black"? How would the farmer from Tay Ninh in VN, Stung Trang in Cambodia or Saravane in Laos know that fact? Just a lucky guess? You must be making a pretty sick joke. Since the "Mortician" stated that the Vietnamese warehoused the remains of U.S. dead from POW camps and crash sites why do we not ask the Vietnamese to give us access to the "warehouse" rather than spending millions excavating another seeded crash site? The silence is deafening on that one.

## A HOUSE DIVIDED

The U.S. government and the private/family groups are divided between those who believe POWS were left behind and those who do not. More sinister is the grouping of those who know we did and, for various reasons do not care. Or, perhaps, they are just flat scared. Then we have the last division within the live POW community itself. With limited resources the fight for money is paramount. There are those who believe any donation buys not only your time but also your support for every bizarre fantasy someone finds on the Internet or dreams up themselves. I have heard people say they have spent millions on this cause; but if they did, their hotels and travel must have been quadruple first class all the way. People clamor for the most recent information those on the ground have. When you become frustrated and just say ENOUGH, you have committed the cardinal sin in the POW community. If people plead with you to give your best guess on when it will all end, you are a fool to predict, and it will come back to haunt you. The government is always watchful, not just to glean any intelligence you might have but to hook-up with whomever you angered today. You either have enough confidence to persevere or you will quit. I believe that all began with the very best of intentions. Then the search is on for the best new innovation, the latest "remote viewer," latest theory or, last but not least, the "Rambo dream." At some point those so enthused about the latest idea for success move on to the latest "flavor of the month." When this happens during a time you are deployed on a combat operation and all the ardent supporters pack up and go back to America, the effect on your morale must be earnestly held in check or you die. More troubling is when people you trust or even love know you are in danger but go ahead with some bizarre action that may very well get you killed. Jealousy runs high, and even causing your death is not out of the question in some quarters. In the end, those who are the most hated and feared by the "They are all dead" lobby are people like Top Holland, Rolling Thunder, Task Force Omega, Run to the Wall etc. They accomplish more in the long run with carefully researched data and a connection to the American people, than I will ever achieve with an agent or a gun. I tip my hat to them all. But we all fit where we belong in this life or we become a loser or a rank wannabe. We all serve our function in trying to beat the clock on a terrible national problem that will one day literally die out. But, except in times of crisis, we are rarely all together in our resolve. We are petty, we are self-thinking and sometimes the POWS are the furthest things from our minds in our individual pursuit of dominance in the "issue." The government loves it as our brethren in prisons die.

If groups do things to each other to dominate the debate, the U.S. government will do its best to arrange your death. When Bo Gritz ran his first mission the VOA and Voice of Liberty announced he and his team were in Laos on their English, Lao and Vietnamese broadcasts. I did not hear it myself and could not believe anyone in government could be so low and cowardly; then it happened to me. In 1987 and numerous times during 1988-89 during two operations into southern Laos, my own government announced I was there and that they had nothing to do with me being there. They even made sure the enemy knew the mission was for POWS. The man brave soldiers had died trying to get out of a place called Loc Ninh, Vietnam in 1972 was offered up a decade and a half later by his own government.

Men and women who sit in offices and cubicles and do not care about deserted Americans are indeed a rare breed of cat. I suppose trying to kill Bo or me was not even the highlight of their day before making their tee time at Fort Meyer.

## POWS

As the publishing of the book by Billy Hendon and Beth Stewart shows, anyone who is truly interested can find the evidence of the crime of abandoning our POWS right in the archives of the U.S. government. What few realize is that disinformation, untrue statements and just plain faulty analysis is left in some archives like "mines and booby-traps" for the uninitiated. Then the perpetrators lie in wait, like frat boys at a toga party, to pounce amid squeals of laughter and giggles. Once again you ask yourself: Who in God's name are these people, and where do they find them? I have no answer to this question. But I am confident the gleeful gremlins at DIA and the retired slugs defending their own past failures in the arena are sharpening their knives of character assassination as I write this. They will go after Billy and Beth. It comes with the territory.

I have participated in and have been a subject of numerous

books. I support letting the public know about the terrible thing that has happened. There may be new congressional committees to investigate, once again, if we knowingly left our POWs in the hands of a cruel and inhumane enemy. Already there are those who are resurrecting the same argument that the enemy only kept them because we did not pay them secretly promised billions in reconstruction aid. This looks good on paper but never did have any real basis in truth. They kept them primarily because they felt we would once again attack them when they started their last assault in 1975. If Richard Nixon was still president in that year it would have been this card they played and reconstruction would not even have been mentioned. They kept them as a "protective shield" and as founts of technical intelligence and data.

Getting us to pay was an idea that came from us and was adopted by them. It was the left wing in America who first demanded that we pay, not POW/MIA activists. The communists picked it up and it became part of their excuse and the lore of the POW Issue. Time and again intelligence came in with those reporting with an untrained eye: "They are teaching how to use and repair U.S. equipment." At the lower level of this, one must only look at what they had Garwood doing: repairing U.S. equipment. He also was shown off to everyone from the Cubans to the PLO. But in the realm of highly trained personnel it reaches a far more sinister level.

## WELCOME TO BAN SAMOY, LAOS

Ban Samoy was for years a training camp and classroom for our enemies from around the world. Air Force pilots were reported to be transferred in twos from a group of four residing in the Xepone area [hub of the Ho Chi Minh Trail], by MI-8 helicopter to and from Ban Samoy. How long has the U.S. government known this? Since 1989, when they intercepted a Federal Express package sent by me to my brother Greg, a police officer in California. Did they cant the satellite and disprove what I said about MI-8 helicopters landing and Americans getting on and off and teaching there? That would be very hard since I had seen them myself—not the Americans but the helicopters coming and going. What would keep them from taking a peek? Most likely it would be students at Ban Samoy and the Russians, together with other Eastern Europeans with the Vietnamese 968 Special Division at Xeno.

There is an almost insane fear of finding anything in Southeast Asia which might require any type of military action. This myth of our inability to deal with such things is the true reason for our refusal to even countenance any type of action in the Asian arena. This was true in 1975 and hampers our ability to combat terrorism today. From POWS to terrorists of world renown, we will not find them in Southeast Asia. Is this because they are not there or is it because we are simply afraid to look? With the most powerful military and supporting technical assets in the world, the answer is in the prior sentence: We are afraid to look!

## HOW HONEST HAS THE GOVERNMENT BEEN?

With some of the personalities involved it is easy to declare the entire history of U.S. government actions on POWS as being some type of "criminal conspiracy" hatched long ago in some back room in Washington, D.C. This has led to a variety of conspiracy theories ranging from the drug trade to the use of young virile Americans to secretly populate Mars so a select few can flee there when the time comes. I see a more benign but much more deadly set of actions put in place for logically "good" if morally reprehensible reasons. Dealing from at least World War II until today, those tasked with dealing with rescuing POWs have, in most cases, viewed it as insurmountable. But rather than just stating this, the lying started and has evolved into a total mythology right down to salted crash sites and a "cooperative" former enemy.

Take photos, for instance. Some of those pictured in the photos are well known to the U.S. government but those government "servants" deny this. The photos are ignored by the government as "not looking like POWs," or missing Americans, and are never released to the press and public. In other cases they are taken out of context to damn a returnee but not released in anything but the cropped version because they damn some who did not return. Garwood is charged with having a weapon in his hands. Not mentioned are other Americans on film with weapons in their hands. The reason is simple in the case of Garwood; the others pictured are dead. Why does this piece of enemy propaganda make Garwood a traitor and the others pictured "dead heroes"? It is simple: He survived and got out of Vietnam. Garwood is constantly called a traitor for signing a single "soldiers appeal." Yet his chief accuser read propaganda every day over the radio in North Vietnam and only stopped because the enemy had not done enough for him. He openly lobbied the enemy as did his wife who joined a so-called "peace group" for early release. Both are major crimes under military law, but the accuser is a retired senior officer, and the PFC is disgraced. Was this so much a punishment for a bad Marine or actually a warning to any others who might make a try to come home?

All photos, our government "servants" say, are blurry and not clear enough for positive ID, yet family members identify them. Are entire American families part of some scam? In some cases the photo of an Asian mountain-man looks very much like the person purported to be a POW in a photo. But why would his hairline be shaved further back to reinforce your case? Then you provide a black-and-white photo instead of the original color one in your files. Why? Because the color photo shows the distinct whiter line of scalp where the hair on top of the "tribesman's" scalp was shaved, to support the government servant's contention. Who scams on this issue?

People of some substance in Asia right up to the present have claimed they saw or even photographed named missing Americans. You would think the polygraph would be the first hurdle. It is the very first question that a U.S. debriefer would ask: "Would you be willing to submit to a polygraph test?" If the answer is yes, the chances of them ever being tested are slim to none because the culture of the public "servants" on this matter is afraid that someone who says, without qualification, "yes," will give away the entire scam of the government not wanting to see anything or know anything. Once that instant "yes" is uttered it is the U.S. government that runs away from the poly. How about doing a routine polygraph on the named U.S. official the source claims to have given photos to? "Out of the question. You cannot challenge this good man's integrity with a polygraph."

Game, set and match: there will be no polygraph test. How low will our government "servant" go? He or she will go as low as it takes to hide the truth. You cannot see one official document on a particular presidential candidate's true military background because he did not sign the standard form allowing it under the Privacy Act. But one who says he feels the evidence supports the survival of POWS had better be ready for anything to be leaked to the press and public.

Even when they leak, they lie. Richard Armitage continued to call Private Garwood a deserter long after he was acquitted of that charge by a military court and it was learned that damage to his jeep and shell casings found at the scene of capture ruled out the desertion charge. Another returned POW had his former wife's statements made about him in a divorce case leaked to the press by the same Department of Defense official, former "Saigon Warrior" Armitage.

When Col. Mike Peck resigned his post as head of the DOD office dealing with the POW question, every rumor and innuendo possible was floated: "You see he talks a lot with his hands." It seems that Peck, the recipient of the Distinguished Service Cross and a bachelor, would have his sexual orientation questioned by the same official. That Peck had a reputation as a bit of a "ladies man" was ignored, because it did not fit the false implication.

Family group leaders and officials right up to the White House are not hesitant to float rumors on any source coming forward. Robin Gregson agreed to come forward to show a video of prisoners in slave labor conditions in Laos, as long as his identity was protected. That did not last the first broadcast of news the morning of the hearing. NSC staff, DOD and the National League of Families executive director all leaked his identity and alluded to his "involvement in a drug case in Thailand." What was his "involvement" in the case? He arranged bail at the request of a defendant, but the leaks made him the defendant in the case. Later the same "honest people" would spread a rumor he was "killed in a drug deal gone bad in New Jersey." Robin died in Lebanon while trying to escape after Gen. Arun lost power.

But I would not wish to paint these people as all bad. After all, Armitage wrote a letter on DOD stationary to support his "friend" from Vietnam when she was arrested for "pandering." The aging Vietnamese beauty with a picture of her and Dick Armitage on a beach together in Vietnam, on her piano, never claimed knowledge of POWs in Vietnam.

How about those troops digging and sifting away at those "crashsites" all over Asia? Men known to have gotten out of their aircraft before it crashed end up somehow in the wreckage, even if they got out miles from the actual crash. This ends the messy business of trying to figure out how they died. We pay handsomely for the privilege of being duped. Few in government have the moral right to speak of honesty on this issue.

## DISHEARTENING THINGS & HOW TO OVERCOME THEM

Probably the most disheartening thing that happens on the issue of missing Americans, if working on the inside, is to go searching for the proverbial "man on a white horse," only to find there is none. Some set out to be that man but end up being intimidated, held up to ridicule or just have their say and fade away. It is a thankless business and any looking for money, personal accolades or just to get their name in print need not apply. Others set out to use the POW Issue as a stalking horse for other things, like running for president. These are usually politicians who soon find out it is a political can of worms that will mark them forever; just ask John McCain. Most set out simply to make a political statement on a "safe issue" and soon rue the day they ever mentioned it. Some soon show their "feet of clay" but more troubling are some that also show a "heart of stone." There are more of these than one could ever imagine and they need to be shunned by all honorable men. Some in government actually come to the conclusion it is best for all concerned to ignore the living POWs because it is a problem which at some point will literally "die out." Others subscribe to the reasoning, as described to me by one of the government's leading lights as a military officer and a civilian: "Any left are like that Navy pilot living on a mountain with that little Laotian girl." Some would be destroyed by such statements, especially a waiting wife. Has the U.S. government ever talked to these people it seems to have enough data on to claim "they wish to be there"? Did they ever talk to Bobby Garwood, a man they claimed to know all about, while he was in Vietnam? I never had one admit to me they had. But even with this professed knowledge, they still had no trouble making all but one dead starting in 1979. Perhaps it is the perceived right they think they have to play God that galls many. "Doctor Death" Kevorkian is a much more honest individual than most of these. At least he admits killing because he believes he is "helping someone to die." Some in government make them dead while wrapping themselves in the flag and claiming to be doing all they can to find and save them: "We get up every morning operating on the assumption that some still survive." HORSE MANURE!

I truly believe there are those who meet each day with great trepidation, hoping this house of cards does not fall on them. They seem to feel no remorse whatsoever at betting against their brother-warrior's ability to even live, let alone maintain honor, a sense of duty, love of family and devotion to their own country. This has brought me to the conclusion that those "servants" working on the POW Issue are far lesser men than those same missing or I will ever be. My recommendations have nothing to do with the appointment of yet another "truth commission." I also do not believe we owe the Vietnamese, Laotians or Cambodians one thin dime. The much talked-about money for reparations was based on North Vietnam and its allies abiding by the agreement made on 27 January 1973. Negotiate with those who hold our men? What somebody in our government thinks of an envoy has no bearing in the Asian scheme of things. That person must have the absolute authority to look them in the eye and tell them the truth: WE KNOW!

In that very same unbalanced moment for the enemy, we should tell him that utter destruction awaits any further hesitation to get down to brass tacks and get our POW Issue resolved. We could even use as a bargaining chip the survival of their new generation and their assets. But we must make clear that we hold them, the older generation, responsible. They have no doubt we have the ability to render their country uninhabitable. We are the most dominant power in history, even if we do not seem to know it. Believe me, for all of their boisterous bull, they know better than any other what we are capable of. They will cave in and trade for simple survival. They know that the Chinese dragon will not help them, and the North Korean nut will fold his tent and not dare interfere. I know few of you believe this, but I have lived among them and fought them for 40 years. Wake up and get it done!

## THE POW ISSUE & THE WAR ON TERROR

If I was ever certain of anything in my life it was that the U.S. government would never deal with anything the way it has our missing warriors. What I did not get is buried in all these statements about "quagmires" and "no more Vietnams." What is the quality that stands out the most between the quest to bring Americans home from foreign shores/captivity and the "war on terror"? It is a simple word; FEAR! In both arenas it appears that too many in the hierarchy and at the nuts and bolts level are scared to death of being accused of missing something they should have known. In preaching leadership we used to give people "the freedom to fail" based on some decision being better than the stuttering "no decision." That no longer seems to be the case. As in the POW Issue, just getting them to take a look at specific real estate in this world is like pulling teeth. They do not cant the satellite; they fight the very idea that something might be where they never thought to look. You can talk until you are blue in the face, assuring them you are not setting them up. Forget it. They will never believe you.

Frankly, this brings into question the entire much-ballyhooed, post Vietnam, leadership environment. Are they truly that used to screwing each other in time of war? I have to tell you, this is a whole new deal. I can think of no prior war where the name-tag ANONYMOUS was the preferred handle. If you are a leader you had best stand out on the battlefield. If you try to be the "gray man" out there, you are in the wrong profession. In the POW realm, for years, faceless "experts" explained away everything that came in. They claimed to be "pursuing every lead." They were not "pursuing"; they were filing. If you think this is not going on today, you are foolish. Of course they will say: "We get up every morning with the assumption, this is the day we (get the named bad guy)." Want to hear the POW version? "We get up every morning operating under the assumption that American POWs are still alive."

I must tell you these two statements are the biggest loads of baloney ever foisted on the American people. Are those running with these balls really this arrogant? No, it is preferable to them if you think that is the case rather than the truth too terrible for them to admit: They are scared to death!

How the heck can you lead soldiers in combat if you are afraid of things written on a darned piece of paper? How can you lead soldiers against the enemy if you are afraid of a picture of the enemy or a POW? Pandering answers are unacceptable in both cases. In the words of SFC Mel McIntire on the *Donahue Show* in 1985 (I paraphrase from memory): "If you are so sure no one is there, why not send us to the riverbank and wait for nobody to show up?" With but a slight variation in wording that same question could be asked today in the terrorism realm. This is not professionally sad; this is the insanity of FEAR. Most become somewhat fearful and apprehensive at times on the battlefield, but there is no place in the arena for those consumed by it. I am sad to report that these are my thoughts.

—MAJ. MARK A. SMITH, U.S. Army, Retired

Note: On December 15, 1985, Smith appeared on *60 Minutes*, together with Gen. Tighe, Rep. Hendon, Robert Garwood and another Green Beret who had filed suit against the Administration. All five men spoke of the government not only making no efforts to investigate sightings, but, in fact, making efforts to hide the facts of sightings and their potential to recover American POWs. Richard Armitage, defending the administrations that failed us in this regard, simply continued the government mantra that "we want more specificity," the cover-up adopted by many presidents.

Before we move on to the next chapter, allow me to introduce you to Tynan Brown, a non-veteran who has taken up the cause of justice for America's POW/MIA families with all his heart and soul. We asked him to write a few words for us.

## TYNAN BROWN

Tynan Brown was supposed to have died long before now, according to hospital personnel, but it appears that God is keeping him around until the POW/MIA Issue is revived in the Congress. He himself is not a veteran, but he has dedicated himself to the servicemen who were still alive after wars and who the government, for political and economic reasons abandoned under the cover of "presumed dead." Tynan ferrets out from some of the most unlikely places information that helps complete the sad picture of government neglect and even malfeasance.

Tynan's father regularly briefed Col. Paul Harkins, who was deputy chief of staff for operations U.S. Third Army-Europe.

## WHO IS TYNAN BROWN?

We asked Tynan to identify himself in his own words, so that those who read this book will know who he is and how he honors all of us with his dedication. Here is the brief message that he sent:

> My name is Ty Brown—nobody important, significant or special in any way, just an average American. I am a disabled former corporate legal

executive. On June 24, 1992 I was 42 years old, unemployed, and appeared to be reasonably healthy. I had been unemployed for 2 and a half years; also, I had just recently become a husband for the first and only time. Then, without any prior signs, I experienced what the total strangers in lab coats called a massive and catastrophic stroke. Unfortunately the late beloved Eileen [Ty's wife, died 2004] was in Mobile, Alabama at the time.

As one of the many consequences of the stroke, I lost the sight in my right eye. As the paralysis and other consequences slowly and gradually started to subside somewhat, I finally met an outstanding doctor I could trust: Dr. Steve Sinatra of Manchester, Connecticut came to my room and introduced himself and said, "It was a bad one but you are not dead and may have some time left."

When I finally returned home a few months later and the late beloved Eileen started to take care of me, it was clear that I would have to learn how to read all over again with one eye instead of two. Eileen took me to a used book sale at the library in Glastonbury, Ct., my left side was still a little paralyzed so I was a bit unsteady walking. I bumped into a table, and a book fell on my foot. The book was *Kiss the Boys Goodbye*, and that was the book I used to teach myself how to read again.

I had never heard of the information in the book from the clueless general news media. In the book there was a reference to the American Defense Institute. I got the phone number and called there. I spoke with a very nice young lady, Vic Leahy, who indicated that she could send more books on the subject. She also indicated that if I became involved in the subject, I would meet the finest people I had ever had the good fortune to meet. By phone she introduced me to Don and Bev Stafford of Colorado, and they introduced to an unusual chap named Maj. Smith. Since that time I have continued to read and research, and help in any way I can.

Then I read the book *Moscow Bound* and on page 151, I noticed a term I had seen before, "Ultra intercepts." During World War II my late father had been a classified Ultra officer on detached service with Third Army Headquarters, and certain things he had told me started to come back. He knew about Operation TICOM and "the Russian fish"; also he knew about the secret Berger codes. It was clear this POW subject was not new in regard to Southeast Asia. Maj. Smith introduced me to some Hmong refugee folks associated with a Catholic church in New England. I have tried to help them with some refugee things. The evaluative comment of Gen. Tighe relative to these humble and honest refugee people is quoted on page 292 of the book *An Enormous Crime*.

I will continue to research and try to help as best I can. I am not a veteran or POW family member, just an unimportant average American. In September, 1992 the suspect folks at Hartford Hospital bluntly advised me that I would probably be dead within 48 hours. Well I am still here, trying to help get the job done. It seems right for a guy who was rather written off by others. Over the years many have been involved, and some have dropped out. As always the news media remains either incompetent or effectively compromised. Let us all pull together to bring justice to our POWs/MIAs. God bless you and America.

—TYNAN BROWN

# SENATE SELECT COMMITTEE ACCUSATIONS OF FRAUD

**THE SENATE SELECT COMMITTEE,** especially those who spent time criticizing and minimizing the testimony of witnesses, voted to investigate a wide range of POW/MIA activists. If the Senate Select Committee found sufficient evidence to investigate alleged instances of "fraud" by POW/MIA activists, then we can say without hesitation that government officials and members of Congress can be charged with fraud for hiding the truth for political or economic reasons. If there is one despicable act that supersedes all other despicable acts attributed to Sen. John McCain in the minds of POW/MIA families it was this. On February 12, 1992, McCain sent a letter to the attorney general of the United States asking for an investigation into possible fraudulent activity by retired Air Force Lt. Col. Jack Bailey, in the case of MIA Donald Carr. Sen. Smith became very concerned. He wrote: "I am not aware of any POW/MIA families who have put forth any allegations with any solid basis that they have personally been victimized by any alleged fraudulent activity, with the exception of dog tag reports out of Southeast Asia (which the DIA has claimed is something which may be orchestrated by the Vietnamese government). . . . Again, if we have more cases of possible fraud, let's send them to the Justice Department. I am confident their trained investigators are in a much better position than our committee to reach a proper determination on these matters. Finally, the legislative history of Senate Resolution 82 makes clear that this Select Committee was created to look into the fate of unaccounted for military personnel from past military conflicts, not to look into the bank accounts of private American citizens. . . . We should not be in the position of having to sub-poena bank records from American citizens on the basis of ru-mors of fraud."

And then, very pointedly, Sen. Smith pointed to what this writer sees as possible traitorous conduct on the part of Staff Di-rector Frances Zwenig during her Hanoi visit. In her discussions with the Vietnamese, she was told that "some U.S. citizens have come up with unfounded issues, and that people—specifically former Congressman Bill Hendon and former Congressman John LeBoutillier—are hurting the . . . interests of the Socialist Republic of Vietnam." They also said, according to the *New York Times*, August 8, 1992, that relations between our two countries had been "taken hostage in the hands of some strong MIA groups."

Ms Zwenig discussed sympathetically with the dictatorial regime that tortured our servicemen, on behalf of the U.S. Sen-ate. This gives a negative impression of POW families and lead-ing members of the select committee who were insisting on POW document transparency. This makes Jane Fonda look like a Bar-bie doll in comparison. At least Jane Fonda was not sent by the U.S. government or a select committee to officially undermine both our POW families and the very members of a U.S. Senate committee who strongly supported them, their rights and their loved ones. Jane Fonda may have done this on her own, but Ms Zwenig was an official representative of a congressional commit-tee. Is it possible that an important member of the committee purposely and deliberately sided with the sentiments of torturers of Americans, against the rights and feelings of POWs and their families? The evidence is right in the committee hearings for all to read. This is not an opinion. It is in black and white.

McCain and Kerry were the two senators that POW/MIA fam-ilies counted on the most. Some of their actions have been very puzzling. For example, McCain described Navy Capt. Eugene "Red" McDaniel (Ret.) as "a fraud and a dishonorable man who preys upon the families of those still unaccounted for in the war." In contrast, journalist Monika Jensen-Stevenson described Mc-Daniel as "one of the most tortured Americans in the history of war." It appears that McCain's famous vitriolic language was unleashed on McDaniel for another puzzling reason. McDaniel had committed, in McCain's eyes, the unpardonable offense of drafting a letter urging that the United States not lift the embargo on Vietnam until they provided a full accounting of all American POW/MIAs. The letter was signed by 50 of his fellow ex-POWs. Shortly thereafter, as a direct result of Sen. McCain's lobbying of other Republican senators, Usry, a distinguished Vietnam veteran, and all other members of the minority staff, who had participated in the POW/MIA investigations, were abruptly fired by Admiral Nance when he became Senator Helm's Chief of Staff.

Sen. Bob Smith, one of the nation's strongest defenders of POW/NIA and their families' rights, sent a memorandum to the Committee Counsel, William Codinha:

**SELECT COMMITTEE ON**
**POW/MIA  AFFAIRS**
**WASHINGTON. DC 20510-4500**
**MEMORANDUM**

TO: William Codinha, Counsel
FROM: Senator Bob Smith, Vice Chairman
DATE: August 25, 1992
RE:  FRAUD

In response to your note to me of August 20th and our recent phone conversations, I have carefully reviewed the committee's activities relating to fraud, along with some recent developments on this issue which concern me.

I want to make the following points in writing to you, so the committee staff and any interested Senators know where I stand on this issue. I also want you to be clear on areas of the investigation on fraud of which I will not approve.

First, activities of the committee's fraud investigation of which I am aware include:

1. In December, 1991, "MIA, Inc - Fraud Investigation- was listed by the counsel as a "TASK" to be looked into by staff investigators.

2. On January 27, 1992, staff investigators submitted an investigative plan to investigate and review allegations of fraud. According to this memo, by this date, staff had already begun to review alleged fraud materials from:

• The files of the House Subcommittee on Asian and Pacific Affairs (the Solarz Committee.)
• The files of the National League of Families.
• The files of the Defense Intelligence Agency and the Department of Defense.
• Magazine and newspaper accounts.

By January 27, 1992, staff investigators had talked to the following people in an effort to gather alleged fraud information

• Major Charles Gittens, POW/MIA Officer at the Office of the Secretary of Defense, International Security Affairs, Department of Defense
• Ann Mills Griffiths and Mary Backley, Directors of the National League of Families, Washington, D.C.
• Pat Rivalgi, POW/MIA Staff Assistant to Congressman Steve Solarz, Chairman of the House Subcommittee on Asian and Pacific Affairs.

3. On January 29, 1992, staff investigators met with the Deputy Director of the Defense Intelligence Agency's POW/MIA Office, Mr. Charles Trowbridge to discuss allegations of fraud.

4. On January 29, 1992, staff investigators sent a formal request to the Internal Revenue Service requesting Form 990 reports from the following sixteen organizations of Vietnam veterans, MIA

family members, and American citizens concerned about the POW/MIA Issue:

National Alliance of Families, American Defense Institute, National Vietnam Veterans Coalition, Veterans of Vietnam War, POW Network, Homecoming II Project, National Forget-Me-Not Association, National League of Families, Voices in Vital America, Viet Now, Task Force Omega, Vietnam Veterans of America, BRAVO, Camp Brandenburg, Operation Rescue, and the Bamboo Connection.

5. On February 12, 1992, staff investigators met Mr. Robert Destatte, Senior Analyst at the Defense Intelligence Agency's POW/MIA Office to collect information on alleged fraud. A letter dated the same day was sent by staff investigators to the Defense Intelligence Agency requesting alleged fraud information mentioned by Mr. Destatte at the meeting earlier in the day.

6. On February 12, 1992, Sen. John McCain, a member of the Select Committee on POW/MIA Affairs, sent a letter to the attorney general of the United States asking for an investigation into alleged fraudulent activity by retired Air Force Lt. Col. Jack Bailey regarding a purported photo of MIA Donald Carr.

7. On February 18, 1992, staff investigators sent a memorandum on the fraud investigation to the counsel. The memorandum states that congressmen Steve Solarz, Ben Gilman and Bob Lagomarsino of the House POW/MIA Task Force wrote the attorney general of the United States on December 21, 1987 concerning P9W/MIA fraud allegations submitted by the Defense Intelligence Agency at the request of Congressman Steve Solarz on October 21, 1987. The memorandum states that the matter was referred by the Justice Depart-

ment to the Chief Postal Inspector in February, 1988, and that "it appears no action was taken."

Committee staff also states in the memorandum that lots of materials have been accumulated from the National League of Families, and that the committee is maintaining files on the following individuals:

Lt. Col. Jack Bailey (USAF-ret.), former POW Captain Red McDaniel (USN-ret.), Lt. Col. Bo Gritz (ret.), former Congressman John LeBoutillier, former Congressman Hendon, former POW Major Mark Smith (ret.), Lt. Col. Al Shinkle (USAF-ret.), State of Tennessee Circuit Judge Hamilton Gayden, Colonel Earl Hopper (USAF-ret.) - father of MIA Earl Hopper, Jr. and former Director of the National League of Families, Ann Griffiths, current Director of the League, and Lamont Gaston of VietNow.

According to the staff file, the 1987 letter to the Attorney General by Solarz, Lagomarsino, and Gilman enclosed financial reports of former Congressman John LeBoutillier (Account for POW/MIA Inc.) and former POW Captain Red McDaniel (American Defense Institute.

As indicated, the Justice Department referred this to the Postal Inspector who did not take any action.

According to a February, 1988 letter to Congressman Stephen Solarz from the Justice Department, if the Postal Inspector had found evidence of a violation of criminal law, it would have been referred to the Justice Department.

This never happened.

On April 1, 1992, staff investigator, former U.S. prosecuting attorney Alex Greenfeld sent a memorandum to the counsel concerning former Congressman Bill Hendon. The memorandum states:

> "I have carefully re-studied the Hendon file.
> There are no allegations with substance of fraud
> or proof of fraud in the file. This includes the
> legal definition and the everyday meaning of the
> word. . . . At this point Hendon can be cleared by
> the Committee of charges of fraud. This would
> clear the air of baseless charges and be an act of
> fairness to Hendon." Less than two weeks after
> writing this memorandum, I note that Alex
> Greenfeld was fired by the counsel. I did not ob-
> ject to this action, as this investigator was selected
> for hire by the Chairman.

I am sure that the reader has already picked up the implication in this letter, i.e., that the investigator, former U.S. prosecuting attorney Alex Greenfeld, was fired because he cleared a Congressman, Bill Hendon, much to the annoyance of the power structure of the Vietnamese government.

I am no constitutional lawyer, but I heavily suspect that this could be a treasonable act, given the nature of the Vietnamese government and what they did to American servicemen, both to those who returned and to those still in custody. Then to head off any possible future fishing expeditions, Smith wrote in his letter to Codinha:

> This new effort by some on the Select Com-
> mittee to search for alleged fraud in the files of
> American citizens who have promoted public
> awareness on this issue is something I do not ap-
> prove of for the following reasons: I am not aware
> of any POW/MIA families who have put forth any
> allegations with any solid basis that they have
> personally been victimized by any alleged fraud-
> ulent activity, with the exception of dog tag re-
> ports out of Southeast Asia (which the DIA has
> claimed is something which may be orchestrated
> by the Vietnamese government.)

## IF NO EVIDENCE, THEN WHAT?

Since no evidence was uncovered that implicated anyone, then what was the purpose of the exercise engaged in by McCain and his Committee allies? A familiarity with Washington politics suggests that intimidation was the goal, intimidation that would make a POW family hesitate before acting for fear that the lack of sensitivity and secrecy already existing with regard to the POWs would extend to the families' daily lives as well. Once again let us call for an inquiry into this matter, with charges being leveled where malfeasance and abuse of senatorial authority are found. The rule of law in this nation will only be respected by coming generations of our youth if they see that power is not a protective wall against punishment for criminal activity. We owe the pursuit of this matter and those two years of hearings to succeeding generations of youth, military or not. The year 2008 is the year when the American people can say "no" to the abuse of power, whether on the Democratic side (Kerry as the model) or the Republican side, (McCain as the model). As mature adults let us seek the truth that beckons us beyond party affiliation. What a wonderful day that would be for America. Now, a few words about Larry Van Renselaar.

## LARRY VAN RENSELAAR

The remains of captured Navy pilot Larry Van Renselaar came home in a body bag, sent back by the North Vietnamese in 1989. This was 20 years after his wife, Diane van Renselaar, had been fighting a losing battle in Washington, attempting to discover Larry's whereabouts. Larry got caught in the crossfire of Washington and Vietnam, as Vietnam was wringing concessions and Washington wanted to end an unpopular war. No one wanted to talk about Larry's case and no one wanted to say where he was being held as a POW. Although they knew that he was still alive and was doing forced labor in a Vietnamese prisoner of war camp, they closed the book on Larry Van Renselaar in 1978 and in spite of evidence to the contrary. Diane continues to seek the truth. Here is what she has to say. "Larry was shot down on September 30, 1968. They closed his case in 1978. In fact, John McCain, who is a very dangerous and violent man, was the driving force behind closing all the POW files, classifying records in order to keep the truth from the families and the American people. McCain is even more dangerous than Bush. I don't want to see this man ever become president, and that's why I want this story out, because he is one of the biggest liars in our government and by no means a friend of the POW families." Diane wonders that if they lied about POWs, how are we to believe what they tell us about "9/11 and the present-day war in Iraq?"

Diane claims that the U.S. government, because they were courting Vietnamese in order to end the war, abandoned thousands of prisoners under the mantra that they were "missing, presumed dead." Like others, she says that it all started with Eisenhower. I don't like to use the word conspiracy, but the picture that is being painted smacks of conspiracy that includes in its web: Eisenhower, Nixon, George W. Bush, John McCain and John Kerry. Diane has been at this problem for more than 30 years. She once attended a gathering of the POW families with the President in 1992, when he was campaigning for president. She recalls the incident very well. "I said straight to his face: 'We can help you get elected if you just tell us the truth about the POWs.' When I told him, again straight to his face, that 'you know Col. Atkins briefed you about many things, including the truth of the POWs,' he looked at me with wide-open eyes, saying nothing, but his jaw literally dropped to the floor." He was unable to reply because Lt. Col. William Atkins had told her that he had briefed Bush many times on the existence of live POWs, and had briefed her on many sordid things he had experienced with Bush. "I talked to Col. Atkins many times about CIA files he had uncovered with Oliver North about John McCain, telling the real truth about McCain's POW captivity. When he and Lt. Col. North got hold of McCain's CIA file" it showed he was out of the system for at least two years, being in an eastern European country instead of being in solitary confinement in a Vietnam jail cell like he has told the public. . . . People need to know the truth about McCain.

He sealed his own records, as well the records of all POWs, so he could continue lying about his POW experience. He was never tortured." Van Renselaar said she discussed McCain with Vietnam POWs in the same camp McCain was held. Larry Larson told her that without a doubt he had not seen McCain for at least a year.

*In closing, we want to present to you two personal testimonies written for this book by Monika Jensen-Stevenson and co-author John Top Holland. Monika, as you have already read, was a noteworthy witness before the Senate Select Committee on POWs/MIAs and author of* Spite House *and* Kiss the Boys Goodbye. *John Top Holland is an American hero in his own right.*

## TESTIMONY OF MONIKA JENSEN-STEVENSON

### THE ONE WHO DIDN'T FADE AWAY

In his farewell speech to Congress on April 19, 1951, Gen. Douglas MacArthur quoted an ancient British ballad "old soldiers never die; they just fade away." And like the old soldier of that song, the general, in his own words, "just faded away, an old soldier who tried to do his duty as God gave him the light to see that duty." Gen. Macarthur was lucky. He lived another 14 years, rich in memories, in the bosom of his family, friends and admirers. At least five to six thousand soldiers who similarly did their "duty as God gave them the light to see that duty" in Vietnam were not so lucky. Most of them were in the prime of life when it was decided for them, that, for the sake of expediency and the honor of those who sent them to fight, they must fade away. Although massive intelligence provided proof that they were alive when peace accords were signed in 1973—many of them were on America's official list of live prisoners expected to return—the U.S. government declared that all live prisoners had been released: Bodies could be negotiated later. Thousands of Americans refused to accept that dictum. More important, those left behind also refused to believe it and through forty some years have valiantly tried to let the world know that they were alive and wanted to come home. The record is full of astoundingly brave and clever efforts made by POWs to signal their government that they were surviving against incredible odds. All of those efforts were thwarted by a bureaucracy, commanded by questionable figures "in charge of the issue" who, under the guise of "secrecy for reasons of national security," weeded and destroyed every document that could challenge the lies propagated by Richard Nixon and Henry Kissinger et al. By the early nineties when through the extraordinary efforts of POW activists and a few good public servants like Senator Bob Smith and Senator Chuck Grassley, a Senate Select Committee was finally established to get at the truth, the office of International Security Affairs put every possible roadblock in front of those staffers who were committed to digging out the truth. (It is no secret that the most powerful Senators on the committee as well as staffers were determined to put the issue to rest once and for all so that the U.S. could open trade negotiations with the former enemy.) When permission was finally granted for staffers to review the files, they had been weeded so thoroughly that not a single paper specifically requested was part of the files. Particularly telling was that all of the documents that listed special codes assigned to airmen (and some others) during the Vietnam War had been destroyed. The codes were meant to be used by those captured to send their own special signal, by, for example, mapping it with stones or stamping it out on grass so that U.S. satellites could pick it up. Such signals were, in fact, recorded by satellites (and confirmed by 97 CIA reports) all through the 1980s in countries like Laos where it was known prisoners were being held. Committed members of Congress like Douglas Applegate (D-Ohio) had investigated these, but International Security Affairs never released the list of special codes, so no crosschecking could be done. Family members of the missing, veterans and some in the intelligence bureaucracy had fought a running battle to examine those files so that comparisons could be made with the satellite data. Naturally, everyone's hopes were high when committee staffers were finally given access to these records only to discover that all files relating to the airmen's codes had been destroyed two years after the war ended. Surviving prisoners who tried to transmit them did so in vain until they died or lost their minds. Some—a very few—might still be trying. Those in charge of the issue for the U.S. government, on the other hand, now had carte blanche in saying that what clearly looked like specialized codes picked up by satellites over Laos, were "photo anomalies" or "shadows and vegetation." In fact, that was their reply even when satellites recorded a stone layout of a known prisoner's boyhood telephone number. This is only one small example of the deliberate and consistent policy on the part of the U.S. government to abandon American prisoners of war in Southeast Asia. Few in the legitimate POW community believe that the reasons for such a policy of deliberate obfuscation, cover-ups and just plain lies on the part of key government players could have any other than a venal reason. Hence the call, as part of this book, for a special prosecutor to look into criminal aspects of the cover-up.

It is mind boggling then, that people who accept that an "enormous crime" has been perpetrated against American POWS, would nevertheless accept the most effective and therefore the most harmful part of that crime: the massive disinformation campaign that the only prisoner who ever made it out of communist Vietnam's hell hole prisons was a traitor who collaborated with the enemy. This campaign has the support of public servants like Presidential candidate John McCain, and numerous creepy operatives who troll the web and deposit filthy [dis]information wherever they can get away with it. Sadly, it is a campaign that seems to be able to enlist (unwittingly or otherwise) even those who claim to have the most comprehensive record on Vietnam POWs and who, at one time, supported Garwood on the basis, they then claimed to have, of proof positive that he has always been innocent. As an example, I quote from *An Enormous Crime* by Billy Hendon, the former congressman who—it is claimed by his supporters—has had access to the most complete record of facts about POWs: "Garwood had become disillusioned with the U.S. effort in South Vietnam. Soon his name began appearing on antiwar leaflets the VC were distributing and a voice believed to be his was heard on Liberation Radio urging U.S. forces to stop fighting. In September 1970, he had been transferred to North Vietnam. He had chosen not to return to the United States when the listed American POWs had been released at Operation Homecoming in 1973."

Ignored in this statement is an entire history of slander against Garwood too long to repeat in this brief essay. Those interested can read my book *Spite House,* a book about which lies also have and continue to be disseminated. (Foremost among the slander is that I was personally forced to pay damages in a legal action that was brought against my publisher and me. I was never personally asked to pay a cent and did not. The book was not withdrawn from bookstores. Large parts of that book came from Bobby Garwood directly (albeit with extraordinary documentation behind them) and I was proud to state this publicly. Like Sen. Smith in his opening statement to the Senate Select Committee on POWs, "I believe Bobby Garwood.")

Just a few documented facts about Bobby Garwood are that there were numerous sightings of him in the prison camps of Vietnam long after he supposedly chose not to return to the United States. South Vietnamese allies who were in the camps with Bobby Garwood after he supposedly "chose not to return to the United States" have testified that he was a prisoner with them in the camps. Contrary to the damaging testimony given at his court-martial by former Americans who had been in earlier camps with him, they describe him as an extraordinary, loyal friend and helpmate in most trying of circumstances. I have a recent photo of them embracing him tearfully at a reunion. Among Garwood's fellow prisoners was none other than South Vietnamese Gen. Lam Van Phat, who was the military commander of the Saigon area until the 1975 collapse who wrote a letter to President Ronald Reagan stating the same. (I interviewed Lam Phat in 1985 after Congressman Hendon provided me with a copy of Lam Phat's letter to President Reagan. To paraphrase *Alice in Wonderland,* this makes the statement, "Garwood had chosen not to return," curiouser and curiouser.

More facts about Garwood's return in 1979 involve the obvious and documented dilemma he created for the U.S. government. He could not be destroyed as easily as an intelligence document, or a satellite "anomaly." He was bona fide proof that the communists had kept prisoners and a living symbol of the thousands of prisoners who had been declared dead by, not only the Nixon administration at Homecoming, but by two congressional commissions that had solemnly accepted communist assurances that "there are no more Americans in Vietnam." Memos from early 1979 in the Jimmy Carter presidential library archives demonstrate that Garwood's status of prisoner and knowledge of others was a chief concern. "Garwood," they state, (claims) that he knows of other Americans who are alive in Vietnam." Publicly the U.S. government denied that Garwood had ever brought up other prisoners. Their motivation for this is made clear in another memo from the same period. "Live Americans (were) a political game" involving the prestige of many high-powered careers. "DIA and State are playing this game," wrote Ms. Michel Oksenberg of the national Security Council to the National Security Adviser on January 21st, 1980. Part of this high-stakes game was to charge Garwood with treason and bring him to court-martial immediately after he left Vietnam.

It was not a game that a Marine Corps private coming out of fourteen years of hell without money or friends could play. To prepare for the court-martial, the government spent millions on an investigation that missed—deliberately or otherwise—the most obvious truths. Garwood was first charged with desertion during the war, a charge that carried the death penalty by firing squad. Yet those who brought these charges knew the facts: Garwood was days away from the end of his Vietnam tour of duty when he disappeared, anxious to see his dying mother and with plans to marry the girl he loved in a double wedding with his best friend just weeks away. It was hardly a time when he would have deserted. During the trial, the prosecution put on the stand Lt. Col. John A. Studds and Charles B. Buchta, who had been Garwood's company commander and battalion motor transport officer at the time of his capture. Both men knew that Garwood disappeared while on an authorized chauffeuring job, yet swore under oath that he had not been authorized to leave. It was a position they had taken from the day Garwood disappeared from the base because they, themselves, broke rules in the way an un-prepared Garwood was ordered to take on a highly dangerous job for which he was not properly armed nor prepared. Having full access to the facts, the prosecution nevertheless took the position that, based on his superiors' false testimony, Garwood had deserted until it was confronted by incontrovertible evidence proving otherwise. To the prosecution's surprise, Billy Ray Conley, one of Garwood's fellow drivers at III MAF, Marine Corps tactical headquarters, voluntarily appeared to testify on Garwood's behalf. He swore that Garwood had, in fact, been on an authorized mission that Conley himself had volunteered for because he wanted Bobby's job after Bobby returned stateside. Conley never forgot that he could have ended up in Bobby's shoes, a fourteen-year prisoner.

If Garwood's court-martial had not been rigged, the obvious perjury of Garwood's III MAF superiors would at the very least have raised serious questions and likely resulted in an acquittal. But such gross miscarriage of justice didn't stop the prosecution from its agenda of trying to destroy the returned prisoner of war who put the lie to their claim that all prisoners were returned. So now, instead of desertion, Garwood was charged with collaborating with the enemy and betraying his fellow Americans. Garwood began to see that he was involved in a process that, for reasons he could not understand, was unwinnable. Exhausted by fourteen years as a prisoner and faced by the total ignominy of being sentenced by the service he had been loyal to through all those years, he withdrew into himself, resigned to his fate.

Suborning perjury, even after this first failure, seems to have been the tactic of choice for the prosecution. Garwood briefly regained hope of getting an acquittal when Col. Tran Van Loc, the communist police chief who sat on a five-man tribunal that had determined his fate in Vietnam along with the fate of other American prisoners, defected to the United States. Tran, because [despite his name,] he was of Chinese descent, fled Vietnam during the border war that broke out between Vietnam and China in the late seventies. The intelligence Tran brought with him—including that on live prisoners—was so important to the U.S. that the DIA's best Vietnamese-language expert and agent, Bob Hyp, was sent to Hong Kong to debrief him. (Hyp would later debrief Garwood. Before his death of a massive heart attack, Hyp sent a message to the author through the editor of *Kiss the Boys Goodbye*, that the debriefing totally vindicated Garwood. Hyp felt Garwood was lucky. Unlike his fellow prisoners, he made it out.) Garwood had never dreamed that vindication could come from a former enemy, but the fact that Tran had defected to the U.S. made it seem possible that he might be willing to tell the truth about Garwood's true prisoner status in Vietnam. Despite the strongest opposition from the prosecutor and the difficulty of getting around Tran's having been assigned to the witness protection program, Garwood's lawyers set up a meeting. When Tran denied knowing Garwood as a prisoner, it destroyed Garwood's hope for any chance at acquittal and lost him the confidence of his own lawyers. More than a decade later, vindication came for Garwood.

Through the relentless work of Sen. Bob Smith, Colonel Tran was again called out of the witness protection program to give sworn testimony before the Senate Select Committee on POWs. Questioned by counsel to the committee Tran described how he had been approached by the government agency that provided both his protection and livelihood, to meet with a military officer who told him to lie about knowing Bobby Garwood. By then, though, Garwood had been so defamed that even Sen. Bob Smith, the vice chairman of the select committee, was unable to bring this the media attention it needed to reopen a public discussion and push for another appeal. (Tran's testimony is in the Senate records, and attorney Vaughn Taylor introduced the evidence vindicating Garwood to the Senate Ethics Committee.)

Suborning the perjury of Tran was not enough for the court-martial prosecution. In order for the American people to be totally convinced that Garwood was not a returning prisoner, he had to be turned into a figure of contempt that no one would believe. It was particularly important to persuade Vietnam veterans many of whom, if not convinced POWs were deliberately abandoned, were nevertheless left with an uneasy feeling that Garwood was being singled out in an unfair way. So the prosecution completely reversed its case. Instead of claiming that he defected, they now claimed that Garwood had been a prisoner after all, albeit one who had collaborated with his captors in ways no other prisoner collaborated.

The kinds of former prisoners subpoenaed to bear witness to this, show clearly just how desperate the prosecution was. Gen. Tighe, former chief of the Defense Intelligence Agency, among many others, questioned whether that fact gave the prosecution undue leverage in the testimony it garnered against Garwood.

According to the *Washington Post* (Dec. 29th, 1979): "All five of the former POWs who testified against Garwood . . . have acknowledged that they collaborated with their captors . . . (they) did whatever their captors were determined to have them do." According to Dr. Edna Hunter, who was chief of the Pentagon's POW unit and debriefed all of the prisoners, none of Garwood's accusers had so much as mentioned bad behavior on his part during their 1973 debriefings. Instead they talked about the suffering they had all endured, Garwood included.

She said, "They were all tortured, tricked and manipulated by the communists." Although she attended the court-martial and wanted badly to testify, she was not called to the stand.

To ensure that Garwood would be convicted somehow, highly questionable allowances were made for some of Garwood's accusers. In at least one instance, the veteran officer who, arguably, gave the most damaging evidence against him was allowed to substitute a written statement for his sworn testimony into the court-martial records. This removed a particularly revealing bit of sworn testimony about physical abuse suffered by Garwood in the camp and gave Garwood's lawyers no opportunity to bring the information before jurors and otherwise help his defense.

With the help of Marine Corps veterans who at one time had access to complete court-martial records, including depositions, I was able to obtain the missing testimony for my files and compare it to the statement in the formal court-marital records.

The issue of other prisoners left behind was not allowed to come before jurors. Garwood's reports about other Americans still in Vietnam, given to Navy Capt. Benjamin R. Ogburn, during a court-ordered psychiatric examination of Garwood, were not allowed as part of the trial. According to the *New York Daily News* of January 23, 1981, "the jurors were not in the courtroom when Ogburn released Garwood's reports about other Americans in Vietnam." In light of the non-existent evidence against Garwood, the jury came back with a minor but nevertheless punishing verdict. He was not to be released by the Marine Corps, but he was not to be paid by them either; he was to be reduced to the lowest rank, forfeiting pay and allowances, including $148,000 due to him for the fourteen years in prison. There was no money to pay his court-martial lawyers, much less to pay for legal experts to question just how the Marine Corps was able to justify this punishment constitutionally or, more important, question the legitimacy of his being tried by a military tribunal in the first place when his tour of duty had ended over a decade before.

He owed hundreds of thousands of dollars in legal bills and began working as a handyman for one of his lawyers to pay him back. He had no money to take care of medical problems arising from the years being imprisoned and tortured, which had taken a vicious toll on his health.

In a policy reminiscent of the former Soviet Union, the United States had turned its one returning prisoner into a non-citizen in his own country. As evidenced by the most recent opus on POWs by Congressman Billy Hendon, who claims to know the facts, the defamation of Garwood continues. Because of the verdict determined by his corrupt court-martial Garwood has no effective means to protest or protect himself. In spite of this, he is still the best evidence that the United States abandoned its prisoners in Vietnam and continues its abandonment to this day. Perhaps not surprisingly, Garwood's true story has somehow made its way across America, some of whose people, in Lincoln's famous words, can be fooled "all of the time, and all of them some of the time. But you cannot fool all of them all of the time."

After my book, *Spite House*, which tells Garwood's story, came out, Garwood and I were invited to speak to more than 200,000 veterans who were assembled near the Vietnam Memorial on Memorial Day, 1998. As they do every year, the veterans and their families traveled from all parts of the country in motorcycle caravans to commemorate and keep alive the concern for unaccounted MIA/POWs. Many gathered there had at one time believed the false propaganda about Garwood put out by the U.S. government. But out of necessity, they educated themselves about the Vietnam War as probably no other group of veterans had ever examined their own war. The had done this by learning from the experiences of those they trusted, their former comrades in arms, whether they had been simple grunts, Special Forces, medics or generals. They wrote letters and published newsletters, using all the electronic means available to them, in which they reprinted every article that dealt with the war in publications across the country. They circulated copies of documents like Garwood's debriefing. Some, like Col. Ted Guy, who, as the highest-ranking officer to have been in charge of POWs at the notorious prison camp called "the Plantation," challenged the increasing number of government hacks who made careers out of debunking intelligence on prisoners abandoned and left behind—particularly intelligence backing Garwood's integrity as a prisoner—a practice they continue today on Internet web sites.

An honor guard of South Vietnamese veterans—some with the rank of general—who had been Garwood's prison campmates embraced him just before he stepped to the podium on Memorial Day, 1998. Emotions began to overwhelm Garwood, as he saluted the crowd, which erupted into wild cheers of "Welcome home," and "We love you Bobby." He continued to salute, unable to speak. The seconds dragged on, the cheering continued, when someone seeing Garwood struggling to speak, spontaneously came out of the crowd. He was a large man, obviously a veteran because of the large metal hook he had for one arm. He put his good arm around Garwood to help hold him up. As Garwood still could not speak, a second man came up from the crowd and supported him from the other side. Then a third man joined them. So embraced, Garwood finally began to speak to the crowd that was suddenly silent, listening intently.

Garwood's speech was short: A few words about the country he loved and the darkness that he knew was not only in his heart but in the hearts of all his fellow veterans; a darkness connected to the brothers they had left behind both dead and alive. Afterward the three men standing with Garwood embraced him.

It was then I noticed the light blue ribbons around the necks of each of the three men who stood with Garwood. Each ribbon held a simple decoration, the American eagle sitting on top of a star; the highest military honor the United States can bestow on a soldier, the Medal of Honor. From the crowd a clear voice said, "Such men do not embrace traitors."

Recently, in a rural area of one of the countries involved in the Vietnam War, I came face to face with a faded human remnant of one of those other abandoned prisoners Garwood wanted so badly to tell us about when he came home in 1979. The man I saw was gaunt, with distinct physical traits and empty blue eyes, reflecting a soul destroyed. Less poetically, one would say that he had been driven out of his mind. Wearing only a loose wrap around his middle, he harmlessly wielded the pickaxe he carried like a weapon mimicking the sound of an M16 as he begged for food. The local women, who threw him scraps of food, shooed him away with looks of disgust and fear. They believe that if they harm someone whose soul has left his body, that soul will haunt them. The faded man spoke to them erratically, in a clearly American accent. Later he crept up to me at an outdoor food stand and stared at me urgently with a face etched in pain and confusion that had flashes of lucidity. He said nothing, and neither did I.

I know though that he wants to come home and very likely could, but there is no chance. I can only imagine for him a fate worse than Garwood's if he does. Most likely, were he to be identified, he would disappear completely. Unlike the women who throw him his daily scraps of food, the country for which he was needlessly sacrificed which calls itself, "indivisible, under God, with liberty and justice for all," is not concerned about being haunted by his spirit.

# Some People Think the POW/MIA Issue Is Over and Done With.

## And John McCain Is One of Them.

## How Wrong They Are . . . .

## Find out what Sen. McCain hopes no one finds out – and much more – in:

# PERFIDY

### *The Government Cabal That Knowingly Abandoned Our Prisoners of War And Left Them to Die*

Most POW/MIA Issue activists are very aware that there are many villainous high ranking government officials who have long been involved in the POW/MIA Issue cover-up. Many of their names are mentioned and their nefarious actions are discussed in this book. However, the majority of the POW/MIA activists, when asked, will quickly tell you that the most detested of these government officials is the one that is most prominent. In the "eyes of the activists" that most villainous person is Senator John McCain. These knowledgeable activists hold total disdain for this person, not only for his alleged felonious collaboration while he was a POW in Vietnam, but the activists are more disgusted with him for his actions while masquerading as "hero" in the Senate. Senator McCain's activities, as noted in the book, are only the small tip of a very large iceberg called "THE POW/MIA ISSUE." In fact, John McCain is very small potatoes when compared to many of the other culprits involved in the cover-up. However, since he is the most prominent of the evil doers he will be used as an example in this advertisement.

Other ex-POWs have spoken of hearing John McCain making radio broadcasts for the North Vietnamese while he was a POW. Thus, it is believed that he did make some (possibly as many as 30) broadcasts for the enemy.

Activists believe McCain gave the enemy military information in exchange for medical care. While sitting as a member of the Senate Select Committee Hearing on the POW/MIA Issue, in 1991-1993, it is believed that Senator McCain misused his position of authority by:

1. Running 'roughshod' over witnesses (i.e: interrupting, disrupting, and belittling) who were recognized as being extremely knowledgeable of the POW Issue, but who had a different perspective.

2. Using the same approach toward POW/MIA family members who testified. McCain brought one of the female witnesses to tears with his deriding and sarcastic remarks.

3. Quickly and voluntarily moving in front of the dais to hug and welcome Mr Bui Tin, a recognized torturer of U.S. POWS. Then Bui Tin was allowed to testify while Major Mark Smith, a retired Special Forces Officer and an ex-POW was denied the same privilege.

On more than several occasions, using questionable maneuvers which are considered "improper by the electorate" but accepted in both houses of Congress, McCain thwarted the wishes of the majority of the American electorate. Twice, McCain added his bills as amendments to other bills under consideration in separate conference committees, to which he had been assigned. McCain's bills had never been before any committee nor had they been discussed on the floor of either house. Thus, McCain thwarted the entire Congress, as well as the will of the concerned American electorate.

On another occasion Senator McCain used his position to usurp the will of the American electorate by clandestinely disrupting a bill that would have nullified one of the apparent malfeasances mentioned above. A House Bill was passed in cloture (with a vote of 410 to 0). This same bill was to be introduced in the Senate, where if it passed without a "nay" would immediately go to the president for signature, which would then become law. McCain could have merely voted "no" on the Senate floor and stopped the cloture vote. Instead he added two amendments prior to Senate vote which stopped the Senate cloture vote, thus killing the bill. In this manner, McCain again thwarted the will of the concerned electorate maintained his phony persona as a friend of the POW/MIA Issue.

Learn, also, how a former abandoned U.S. POW was endangered AGAIN through McCain's action. This former POW was asked to join a Congressional junket to Vietnam to pinpoint where he had witnessed other abandoned POWs. Because of McCain's misplaced torridity, diplomatic immunity was denied to this volunteer. This former abandoned-POW still chose to be part of the junket, thus endangering his well-being (with nearly disastrous results) for the benefit of other abandoned POWs.'.

Who is Heroic and who does dastardly deeds?

**THIS BOOK WILL TELL YOU WHO ALLOWED THIS!**

**THIS BOOK WILL TELL YOU WHAT THEY DID!**

**THIS BOOK WILL TELL YOU WHERE THEY DID THIS!**

**THIS BOOK WILL TELL YOU WHEN THEY DID TIIIS!**

**THIS BOOK WILL TELL YOU HOW IT WAS DONE!**

**PERHAPS YOU CAN FIGURE OUT WHY THEY DID THIS !**

**AN INDEPENDENT COUNSEL IS NEEDED  TO INVESTIGATE THE POW/MIA ISSUE AND JOHN McCAIN'S ROLE IN COVERING UP THE TRUTH!**

**TO ORDER THIS BOOK CALL AFP** toll free at 1-888-699-NEWS (6397) and charge your copy(s) to Visa or MasterCard. Send payment for book to AFP, 645 Pennsylvania Avenue SE, Suite 100, Washington, D.C. 20003 using the handy order form at the back of this book. See www.americanfreepress.net for more. No charge for shipping & handling inside the U.S.

**PRICES: $25 for one copy.**

**$48 for two copies ($24 each).**

**$69 for three copies ($23 each).**

**$88 for four copies ($22 each).**

**$105 for five copies ($21 each)**

**Six or more copies are just $20 each.**

Carton prices available. Call 202-544-5977.

**U.S. MILITARY VETERANS/ACTIVES TAKE 25% OFF ABOVE PRICES (UP TO FIVE COPIES).  HELP GET THE WORD OUT!**

*PHANTOM FLIGHT 93 and Other Astounding September 11 Mysteries Explored.* By Victor Thorn and Lisa Giuliani. A collection of interviews, articles and on-the-scene investigations by Thorn and Giuliani expose the government cover-up of the fate of Flight 93 (the Shanksville flight) as pure fiction. What really happened? Softcover, 150 pages, #1575, $20.

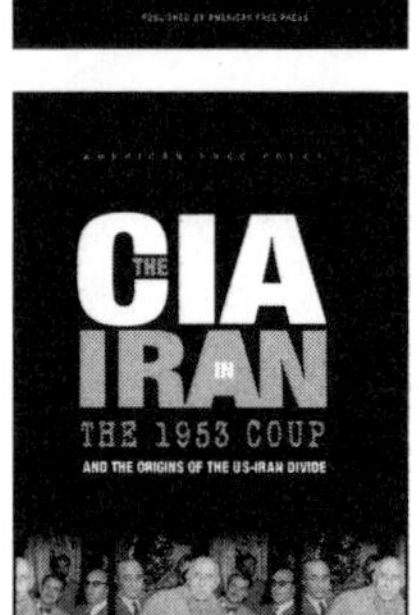

*THE CIA IN IRAN: The 1953 Coup & the Origins of the US-Iran Divide* reveals how U.S. and British operatives employed every dirty trick at their disposal, including bribery, murder and terrorism, to topple the democratically elected government of Prime Minister Mohammad Mossadeq and maneuvered the infamous Shah of Iran into power. Softcover, 150 pages, #1575, $20.

*JIM TUCKER'S BILDERBERG DIARY*
AFP editor and reporter Jim Tucker has spent the last 25 years tracking down a group of the richest and most influential industrialists, bankers, media moguls and world leaders that meets every year in complete secrecy in some of the poshest venues the world has to offer. Only Tucker has penetrated these meetings and reported on the nefarious goings on inside despite armed guards, attack dogs and barbed wire fences. Softcover, 272 pages, $25.

*DEBUNKING 9-11: 100 Unanswered Questions About September 11*
All of AFP's groundbreaking coverage of the event from the beginning: the spies operating in New York; the many theories put forth by independent researchers who reject the government's explanation of many of the events of Sept. 11; alternative theories as to why the twin towers collapsed; detailed information of foreknowledge by the government and foreign intelligence agencies; and much, much more. Large-sized (8.5" x 11" format), 108 pages, $20. Photos.

*SUPPRESSED SCIENCE: Radiation, Global Warming, Alternative Health & More*
Scientist Jack Phillips imparts his lifelong wisdom on a number of suppressed scientific topics including suppressed cancer cures, persecuted alternative health practitioners, the beneficial effects of radiation, the health hazards of vaccines, the real cause of the autism epidemic, the use of divining rods as unexplained—but real—science, and more. Softcover, 125 pages, 176, $17.

*FINAL JUDGMENT: The Missing Link in the JFK Assassination Conspiracy*
This is the controversial underground best seller by Michael Collins Piper documenting the heretofore untold role of Israel's intelligence service, the Mossad, in the assassination of John F. Kennedy because of JFK's steadfast determination to stop Israel from building an arsenal of nuclear weapons of mass destruction. Softcover, 768 pages, 1,000+ footnotes, $25.

*THE HIGH PRIESTS OF WAR: The Secret History of America's Neo-Cons*
*The High Priests of War,* by Michael Collins Piper, tells the secret history of how America's neo-conservatives came to power and orchestrated the war against Iraq as the first step in their drive for global power. Softcover, 144 pages, $20.

*DIRTY SECRETS: Crime, Conspiracy & Cover-Up During the 20th Century*
Here's a fascinating collection of writings from Michael Collins Piper, transcripts of uncensored radio interviews and reviews of his works—all compiled in one volume. Read where Piper's investigations have led him on such explosive topics as the Martin Luther King and JFK assassinations, the Oklahoma City bombing, the attack on the *Liberty* and many more. Softcover, 256 pages, $22.

*THE NEW JERUSALEM:*
*Zionist Power in America*
This explosive study contains all of the solid facts and figures documenting the massive accumulation of wealth and power by those who have used that influence to direct the course of American affairs—the forces behind America's "New Imperialism." While there are many historical books on "the Israeli lobby," this is unique. Another classic by Michael Collins Piper. Softcover, 184 pages, $20.

*FUTURE FASTFORWARD:*
*Zionist Anglo-American Empire Meltdown*
Is global "Empire Capitalism" about to come crashing down? Will there be a worldwide "people's war" against the Zionists and their powerful minions? Is nuclear war inevitable? What retribution will be meted out to those people who have foisted New World Order slavery upon the people of the world? By Asian political figure Matthias Chang. Softcover, 400 pages, $25.

*BRAINWASHED FOR WAR:*
*Programmed to Kill*
From the Cold War to Vietnam and now the so-called "War Against Terror" we have been lied to, mind-controlled and duped by a power elite with the goal of making us mindless supporters of bloody war. Also by Matthias Chang. Softcover, 556 pages, $30.

*GEORGE WASHINGTON'S Speeches & Letters:*
Here's an inspiring collection of 19 of our first president's most private writings and powerful speeches to friends, family members and colleagues. Includes Washington's Farewell Address and his Farewell to the Army. Letters include ones to his wife, his mother, Gen. Braddock, members of the Continental Congress and more. 12 illustrations. Softcover, 256 pages, $13.

*NO BEAUTY IN THE BEAST:*
*Israel Without Her Mascara*
Author Mark Glenn examines Israel from a politically incorrect perspective and comes to the conclusion that the beast of John's Revelation is in fact the beast of Zionist supremacy—a beast that is now devouring the world. Also an amazing chapter of quotes from the perpetrators themselves. Must read for all who call themselves Judeo-Christians. Softcover, 302 pages, $25.

*THE PASSION PLAY AT OBERAMMERGAU*
*How the Thought Police Succeeded in Altering*
*The World's Oldest Passion Play*
Find out how the German citizens of Oberammergau, Germany, were forced by the Zionist thought police to change their Passion Play—performed since the 1600s—to make it "less offensive." A shocker. Includes the full text of the play in novel form. Softcover, 225 pages, $20. Many photos.

*THE CITIZENS HANDBOOK:*
*Pocket-Sized Patriotic Primer for All Ages*
Contains the full text of the Declaration of Independence, Constitution, Bill of Rights and ALL subsequent amendments plus a section on every American's rights when called for jury duty. Full color varnished cover to increase life. Pocket-sized softcover, 80 pages, $5. More than 50,000 distributed.

*FDR: THE OTHER SIDE OF THE COIN:*
*How We Were Tricked Into World War II*
The author, Rep. Hamilton Fish, felt that had FDR listened to public opinion, millions of lives would have been spared. He documents how FDR refused every prewar peace concession and later refused peace initiatives from anti-Hitler Germans. Mr. Fish traces the roots of the Korean and Vietnamese conflicts to the territorial concessions made by FDR to Stalin at Yalta. Softcover book, 255 pages, $20.

SUBSCRIBE TO *AMERICAN FREE PRESS* NEWSPAPER AND GET FREE BOOKS!

## AMERICAN FREE PRESS ORDERING COUPON

| Item# | Description/Title | Qty | Cost Ea. | Total |
|---|---|---|---|---|
|  |  |  |  |  |
|  |  |  |  |  |
|  |  |  |  |  |
|  |  |  |  |  |
|  |  |  |  |  |
|  |  |  |  |  |
|  |  |  |  |  |
|  |  |  | SUBTOTAL |  |
| S&H: No S&H inside U.S. Outside U.S. add $6 per book | | | |  |
| Send a 1-year subscription to AFP for $59 plus 1 free book* | | | |  |
| Send a 2-year subscription to AFP for $99 plus 2 free books** | | | |  |
|  |  |  | TOTAL |  |

***NOTE ABOUT FREE BOOKS:** For a one-year subscription to *American Free Press* newspaper ($59), we'll send you one free copy of Michael Collins Piper's *The High Priests of War*. ****For a two-year subscription we'll send you *The High Priests of War* PLUS *The New Jerusalem: Zionist Power in America*—almost $40 in free books! (Domestic USA only.)**

**PAYMENT OPTIONS:** ❑ CHECK/MO  ❑ VISA  ❑ MASTERCARD

Card # ___________________________________________________

Expiration Date _________________ Signature _______________

POW38

**CUSTOMER INFORMATION:**

NAME _______________________________________________________

ADDRESS ____________________________________________________

City/STATE/ZIP ______________________________________________

**RETURN WITH PAYMENT TO:** AMERICAN FREE PRESS, 645 Pennsylvania Avenue SE, Suite 100, Washington, D.C. 20003. Call 1-888-699-NEWS (6397) toll free to charge a subscription or books to Visa or MasterCard.